SUPPORT TO THE DOD CYBER WORKFORCE ZERO-BASED REVIEW

Developing a Repeatable Process for Conducting ZBRs within DoD

Molly F. McIntosh, Sasha Romanosky, Thomas Deen, Samantha E. DiNicola,
Christopher Ferris, Jonathan Fujiwara, Priya Gandhi, Henry Hargrove,
Kirsten M. Keller, Maria C. Lytell, Mace Moesner IV, Isabelle Nazha,
Zhan Okuda-Lim, Nina Ryan, Karen Schwindt, Amanda Wicker

Prepared for the Department of Defense Chief Information Office
Approved for public release; distribution is unlimited

For more information on this publication, visit **www.rand.org/t/RRA660-6.**

About RAND

The RAND Corporation is a research organization that develops solutions to public policy challenges to help make communities throughout the world safer and more secure, healthier and more prosperous. RAND is nonprofit, nonpartisan, and committed to the public interest. To learn more about RAND, visit www.rand.org.

Research Integrity

Our mission to help improve policy and decisionmaking through research and analysis is enabled through our core values of quality and objectivity and our unwavering commitment to the highest level of integrity and ethical behavior. To help ensure our research and analysis are rigorous, objective, and nonpartisan, we subject our research publications to a robust and exacting quality-assurance process; avoid both the appearance and reality of financial and other conflicts of interest through staff training, project screening, and a policy of mandatory disclosure; and pursue transparency in our research engagements through our commitment to the open publication of our research findings and recommendations, disclosure of the source of funding of published research, and policies to ensure intellectual independence. For more information, visit www.rand.org/about/research-integrity.

RAND's publications do not necessarily reflect the opinions of its research clients and sponsors.

Published by the RAND Corporation, Santa Monica, Calif.

Library of Congress Cataloging-in-Publication Data is available for this publication.

ISBN:978-1-9774-0951-5

Cover images: Pentagon: Ekarath/Getty Images. Data: Dario Fogo/Getty Images.

Cover design: Rick Penn-Kraus.

About This Report

In the fiscal year 2020 National Defense Authorization Act (NDAA), the U.S. Department of Defense (DoD) is tasked with performing a zero-based review (ZBR) of its cyber and information technology (IT) personnel. The NDAA requires that DoD departments, components, and agencies complete ZBRs for their cyber and IT workforces and that those ZBRs be submitted to the Principal Cyber Advisor (PCA), DoD Chief Information Officer (DoD CIO), and the Under Secretary of Defense for Personnel and Readiness (USD P&R).

DoD CIO asked the RAND Corporation's National Defense Research Institute (NDRI) to produce a transparent and repeatable process for validating and ensuring the consistency of data and analysis used for the ZBR. The scope of this RAND study includes ten organizations selected from across the four DoD services—the U.S. Air Force, Army, Marine Corps, and Navy—plus the Defense Information Systems Agency. This report describes the methods used in the repeatable process and summarizes our findings across the ten organizations that were selected to participate in the DoD cyber ZBR.

RAND National Security Research Division

This research was sponsored by the Principal Advisor for Cybersecurity, Strategy, Planning, and Oversight in the Office of the DoD CIO and conducted within the Forces and Resources Policy Center of the RAND National Security Research Division (NSRD), which operates the National Defense Research Institute (NDRI), a federally funded research and development center sponsored by the Office of the Secretary of Defense, the Joint Staff, the Unified Combatant Commands, the Navy, the Marine Corps, the defense agencies, and the defense intelligence enterprise.

For more information on the RAND Forces and Resources Policy Center, see www.rand.org/nsrd/frp or contact the director (contact information is provided on the webpage).

Acknowledgments

We are grateful to the DoD Tri-Chair Action Officers (AOs)—Walter Spears, Elizabeth Hocker, and Hali Sparks of DoD CIO; Christi Johnson, Bety Idriss, Jacklyn Nelson of PCA; and Curtis Smolinsky of USD P&R—and to the members of the DoD cyber ZBR AO working group for their valuable feedback and guidance. We would also like to thank our RAND colleagues, Beth Seitzinger and Zev Winkelman; our quality assurance reviewers, Igor Mikolic-Torreira, Tracy Krueger, and Craig Bond; and the DoD interview and data call participants.

Summary

Section 1652 of the fiscal year 2020 National Defense Authorization Act (NDAA) tasks the U.S. Department of Defense (DoD) to perform a *zero-based review* (ZBR), defined as a "review in which an assessment is conducted with each item, position, or person costed anew, rather than in relation to its size or status in any previous budget" (Pub. L. 116-92, 2019). The NDAA requires that DoD departments, components, and agencies complete ZBRs for their cyber and information technology (IT) workforces and that those ZBRs be submitted to the Principal Cyber Advisor (PCA), DoD Chief Information Officer (DoD CIO), and Under Secretary of Defense for Personnel and Readiness (USD P&R), which are collectively referred to as the Tri-Chair. The Tri-Chair, in turn, is tasked with reviewing and certifying the ZBR submissions, providing recommendations based on the findings, overseeing the implementation of those recommendations, and communicating the results of the overall ZBR effort to Congress.

DoD CIO asked RAND's National Defense Research Institute to produce a transparent and repeatable process for validating and ensuring the consistency of data and analysis used for the ZBR. The process began by organizing requirements from the NDAA into five themes: current workforce, current work performed, manning and capability gaps, potential barriers to efficiency and effectiveness, and potential future changes in work performed or requirements.

Next, to address each theme, we applied both quantitative and qualitative research methods, using multiple data sources, such as

- an analysis of workforce data based on the DoD CIO Workforce Census and email distribution lists generated by selected DoD organizations (described below) to identify and communicate with the cyber and IT workforces
- subject-matter expert (SME) interviews with leadership and supervisors at the selected organizations
- a RAND-designed data call that was issued by DoD to the selected organizations
- virtual deskside interviews with a small number of staff at the selected organizations
- a literature review and analysis of data comparing DoD and private sector cyber workforces
- an analysis of a sample of cybersecurity and IT civilian position descriptions (PDs) provided by the selected organizations.

We then mapped each method and data source to the themes as shown in Table S.1.

TABLE S.1
Mapping Methods and Data Sources to Themes

Theme	Method or Data Source					
	Analysis of DoD Workforce Data	SME Interviews	Work Analysis Data Call	Deskside Interviews	Comparison of DoD and Private Sector Cyber Workforces	Analysis of Civilian PDs
Current workforce	X					X
Current work performed			X	X		
Manning and capability gaps		X		X	X	
Potential barriers to efficiency and effectiveness		X	X	X		
Potential future changes to work performed or requirements		X		X		

This study includes a select number of organizations across the four DoD services—the U.S. Air Force, Army, Marine Corps, and Navy—plus the Defense Information Systems Agency (DISA). In addition, our research approach was guided by the Tri-Chair's decision to focus the ZBR on two of the functional areas in the DoD Cyber Workforce Framework (DCWF): cybersecurity and IT.

In this report, we present our findings, aggregated across the participating organizations and organized by theme. Overall, organizations that participated in the DoD cyber ZBR reported a total of almost 18,000 cybersecurity and IT personnel, 84 percent of whom are civilians and 16 percent of whom are military personnel.

Our analysis of almost 200 PDs suggests that the selected organizations are still working to align their hiring practices (as expressed through PDs) with DoD's adoption of the DCWF taxonomy of cybersecurity and IT positions. For example, we find that 16 percent of PDs were clearly and uniquely mapped to a unique DCWF work role, while about 20 percent of PDs mapped to multiple DCWF work roles and about 20 percent of PDs did not map to any DCWF work role.

Furthermore, the data call responses of personnel across the selected organizations suggest that most personnel perform their cybersecurity and IT tasks weekly or monthly, and they typically view these tasks as being very important to their individual job performance.

By comparing the selected DoD and private sector cybersecurity and IT workforces, we find that the participating DoD organizations have approximately 2.5 times the number of personnel allocated to basic IT functions, relative to such personnel in the private sector. And yet, these participating DoD organizations still experience personnel gaps for these basic IT functions at much higher percentages than in the private sector. Moreover, private sector organizations appear to experience much higher rates of personnel gaps for cybersecurity work roles, relative to gaps in the selected DoD organizations.

We captured issues related to work efficiency and effectiveness through interviews with DoD cyber and IT personnel, who cited military processes, access to technology, and budget as being the leading constraints to their efficiency and effectiveness.

Finally, we note that the ZBR process described in detail in this report and augmented by a series of instrumental actions taken by representatives from the Tri-Chair organizations, the services, and DISA provides a framework that DoD can use to continue to conduct ZBRs across the DoD cyber enterprise.

Contents

Figures and Tables

Figures

Tables

CHAPTER ONE

Introduction

Section 1652 of the fiscal year (FY) 2020 National Defense Authorization Act (NDAA) tasks the U.S. Department of Defense (DoD) to perform a zero-based review (ZBR) of its cyber and information technology (IT) workforces; this ZBR is to include reviewing workforce data and conducting interviews with DoD cyber personnel to characterize the existing cyber workforce (Pub. L. 116-92, 2019). A *ZBR*, as defined in the NDAA, is a "review in which an assessment is conducted with each item, position, or person costed anew, rather than in relation to its size or status in any previous budget" (Pub. L. 116-92, 2019). Specifically, the NDAA requires that DoD departments, components, and agencies complete ZBRs for their cyber and IT workforces and that those ZBRs be submitted to the Principal Cyber Advisor (PCA), the DoD Chief Information Officer (DoD CIO), and the Under Secretary of Defense for Personnel and Readiness (USD P&R), which are collectively referred to as the Tri-Chair. The Tri-Chair, in turn, is tasked with reviewing and certifying the ZBR submissions, providing recommendations based on the findings, overseeing the implementation of those recommendations, and communicating the results of the overall ZBR effort to Congress.

The overall DoD cyber ZBR approach was, in part, informed by past efforts, such as the zero-based budgeting (ZBB) process introduced in 1970,[1] the U.S. Army's "Night Court" process in 2019 (Daniels, 2019), and the FY 2021 Defense-Wide Review (Office of the Secretary of Defense, 2020). In addition, the U.S. Navy and the U.S. Marine Corps conducted ZBRs in 2012 and 2019 (Navy Cyber ZBR Task Force, 2012; Vintun, 2019a; Vintun, 2019b; Vintun, 2019c), respectively, which each focused on their cyber workforces to determine the appropriate staffing, resources, skills, and training that would be necessary to fulfill their cyber missions.

The scope of the DoD cyber ZBR effort was focused on a select number of participating DoD organizations, specifically

- **Marine Corps:** Marine Corps Cyberspace Operations Group, Marine Corps Installations West (MCIWEST), and 1st Network Battalion (1st Network Bn)

[1] ZBB is a methodology first proposed by Peter Pyhrr in 1970 as a rigorous yet qualitative budgeting process, designed to evaluate the typically service- and support-oriented activities performed at Texas Instruments, while other budgeting approaches at the time were designed to evaluate manufacturing activities (Pyhrr, 1970).

- **Army:** Army Cyber Command—including Network Enterprise Technology Command—and Communications-Electronics Command
- **Air Force:** Air Force Materiel Command
- **Navy:** Naval Information Warfare Systems Command and Naval Network Warfare Command
- **Defense Information Systems Agency (DISA):** operations center; development and business center; Cloud Computing Program Office; Joint Force Headquarters–Department of Defense Information Network (JFHQ-DODIN); joint service provider; administrative control organizations (including the White House Communications Agency, Joint Artificial Intelligence Center, Secretary of Defense Communications, and White House situation support staff); mission support organizations (including Risk Management Executive, Procurement Services Directorate, and Workforce Services and Development Directorate); Inspector General; and Joint Staff Support Center.

Moreover, the DoD cyber ZBR effort focuses on two functional areas from the DoD Cyber Workforce Framework (DCWF) (DoD, 2020): cybersecurity and IT.[2] The DCWF is the DoD cyber taxonomy based on the National Initiative for Cybersecurity Education (NICE) Cybersecurity Workforce Framework and DoD Joint Cyberspace Training and Certification Standards.[3] The cybersecurity and IT functional areas, and their associated workforces, are defined in the DCWF as follows:

> *Cybersecurity.* Personnel who secure, defend, and preserve data, networks, net-centric capabilities, and other designated systems by ensuring appropriate security controls and measures are in place, and taking internal defense actions. This includes access to system controls, monitoring, administration, and integration of cybersecurity into all aspects of engineering and acquisition of cyberspace capabilities.
>
> *IT (cyberspace).* Personnel who design, build, configure, operate, and maintain IT, networks, and capabilities. This includes actions to prioritize, implement, evaluate, and dispose of IT as well as information resource management; and the management, storage, transmission, and display of data and information. (DoD Cyber Exchange Public, undated-b)

Table 1.1 shows the 25 DCWF work roles (with the work role number in parentheses) that fall under the cybersecurity and IT functional areas. These 25 work roles are the focus of this report and the DoD cyber ZBR.

---

[2] There are a total of five functional areas described by the DCWF: IT, cybersecurity, cyberspace effects, intelligence (cyberspace), and cyberspace enablers (DoD Cyber Exchange Public, undated-b).

[3] For more information on the DCWF and the cybersecurity and cyberspace IT functional areas and work roles, see DoD Cyber Exchange Public, undated-b; DoD Cyber Exchange Public, 2020a; and DoD Cyber Exchange Public, 2020b.

TABLE 1.1
DCWF Cybersecurity and IT Work Roles

Cybersecurity Work Roles	IT Work Roles
• Cyber Defense Forensics Analyst (212) • Systems Security Analyst (461) • Cyber Defense Analyst (511) • Cyber Defense Infrastructure Support Specialist (521) • Cyber Defense Incident Responder (531) • Vulnerability Assessment Analyst (541) • Authorizing Official/Designating Representative (611) • Security Control Assessor (612) • Secure Software Assessor (622) • Information Systems Security Developer (631) • Security Architect (652) • Information Systems Security Manager (722) • Communications Security (COMSEC) Manager (723)	• Technical Support Specialist (411) • Database Administrator (421) • Data Analyst (422) • Knowledge Manager (431) • Network Operations Specialist (441) • System Administrator (451) • Software Developer (621) • Systems Developer (632) • Systems Requirements Planner (641) • Enterprise Architect (651) • Research and Development Specialist (661) • System Testing and Evaluation Specialist (671)

SOURCE: DoD Cyber Exchange Public, 2020a; DoD Cyber Exchange Public, 2020b.

NOTE: DCWF work role numbers are shown in parentheses.

As a member of the Tri-Chair, DoD CIO asked RAND's National Defense Research Institute (NDRI) to conduct research in support of the ZBR and, in particular, to produce a transparent and repeatable process for validating and ensuring the consistency of data and analysis used in the ZBRs. As a result, we wrote five unpublished reports—one for each of the four DoD services and DISA—to outline organization-specific findings that could be used in the writing of their ZBR submissions. We aggregate and present the findings from these unpublished reports here.

In the remainder of this report, we discuss the data sources and analytical methods that we used, present our findings organized around five major themes—current workforce, current work performed, manning and capability gaps, potential barriers to efficiency and effectiveness, and potential future changes in work performed and requirements—and close with a summary discussion of the repeatable ZBR process, which DoD can use to continue to conduct ZBRs across the DoD cyber enterprise.

CHAPTER TWO

Methods and Data Sources

The development of a transparent and repeatable process for the DoD cyber ZBR was guided first and foremost by the language of the FY 2020 NDAA requirements. The key tasks required by Section 1652 are summarized in Table 2.1, organized by the "scope of review" and "elements" subheadings found in the NDAA.

We organized these 12 key tasks into five themes (see Table 2.2): current workforce, current work performed, manning and capability gaps, potential barriers to efficiency and effectiveness,[1] and potential future changes in work performed or requirements.

To address these themes, we employed both quantitative and qualitative research methods and leveraged the following multiple data sources:

- an analysis of workforce data collected from a workforce census issued by DoD CIO and email distribution lists created by the selected organizations used to identify and communicate with cybersecurity and IT personnel
- interviews with subject-matter experts (SMEs), specifically leadership from the selected organizations, as well as supervisors who oversee the cybersecurity and IT workforces at the selected organizations
- an analysis of a RAND-designed data call, issued by DoD to all cybersecurity and IT personnel at the selected organizations
- virtual deskside interviews with a small number of cybersecurity and IT staff at the selected organizations to aid in our interpretation of the data call results
- a literature review and analysis of data comparing the DoD and private sector cyber workforces
- an analysis of a sample of cybersecurity and IT civilian position descriptions (PDs) provided by the selected organizations.

These methods and data sources, which form the basis of the repeatable ZBR process, are described in more detail below. In this chapter, we discuss DoD organizations in the order in which they participated in the ZBR: Marine Corps, Army, Air Force, Navy, and DISA.

---

[1] In the protocols created for this study, we defined *efficient* as leading to the least amount of waste and *effectiveness* as successfully producing the desired result.

TABLE 2.1
Key Tasks from Section 1652 of the FY 2020 NDAA

Task	Description
Scope of review	
c1	Assess military, civilian, and contractor positions and personnel performing cyber and information technology missions.
c2	Determine the roles and functions assigned by reviewing existing PDs and conducting interviews to quantify the current workload performed by military, civilian, and contractor workforces.
c3	Compare DoD's manning with the manning of comparable industry organizations.
c4	Include evaluation of the utility of cyber and IT-focused missions, positions, and personnel within such components • to assess the effectiveness and efficiency of current activities • to assess the necessity of increasing, reducing, or eliminating resources • to guide prioritization of investment and funding.
c5	Develop recommendations and objectives for organizational, manning, and equipping change, accounting for anticipated developments in information technologies, workload projections, automation and process enhancements, and DoD requirements.
c6	Develop a gap analysis, contrasting the current organization and the objectives developed in task c5.
c7	Develop roadmaps of prioritized activities and a timeline for implementing the activities to close the gaps identified in task c6.
Elements	
d1	Determine whether PDs and coding designators for given cybersecurity and IT roles are accurate indicators of the work being performed.
d2	Determine whether the function of any cybersecurity or IT position or personnel can be replaced by acquisition of cybersecurity or IT products or automation.
d3	Determine whether a given component or subcomponent is over- or under-resourced in terms of personnel, using industry standards as a benchmark where applicable.
d4	Determine whether cybersecurity service provider positions and personnel fit coherently into the enterprise-wide cybersecurity architecture and with DoD's cyber protection teams.
d5	Determine whether the function of any cybersecurity or IT position or personnel could be conducted more efficiently or effectively by enterprise-level cyber or IT personnel.

SOURCE: Pub. L. 116-92, 2019.

DoD Workforce Data

Data concerning the counts of requirements and personnel (i.e., workforce data) used in this report come from two sources: the DoD CIO Workforce Census and email distribution lists generated by the selected organizations.

In September 2020, DoD CIO tasked each of the selected organizations with providing a census of their cybersecurity and IT workforces. Specifically, the DoD CIO Workforce Census captured the number of personnel and requirements by DCWF work role in the cybersecurity and IT functional areas, with separate counts for civilian and military person-

TABLE 2.2
Key Tasks from Section 1652 of the FY 2020 NDAA Mapped to Themes

Theme	Key Tasks Mapped to This Theme
Current workforce	c1, d1
Current work performed	c2
Manning and capability gaps	c3, c6, c7, d3
Potential barriers to efficiency and effectiveness	c4, d5
Potential future changes in work performed or requirements	c5, d2, d4

SOURCE: Authors' analysis of the tasks in Section 1652 of the FY 2020 NDAA (Pub. L. 116-92, 2019).

nel, as well as the number of contractors, by type, per the Department of Defense Manual (DODM) 8570.01, 2015.

We also collected workforce data from the email distribution lists generated by the selected organizations, which they used to identify and communicate with cybersecurity and IT personnel at the selected organizations.

Subject-Matter Expert Interviews

To better understand the organizational context and to develop a high-level understanding of the workforce and its workload, we conducted interviews with leadership or supervisors (i.e., SMEs) in each of the selected organizations. Each organization nominated a representative who worked with us to identify SMEs from their organization who would participate in the interviews.

Considerations for SME selection included direct knowledge and experience with the organization's cybersecurity and/or IT missions and with the management of one or more such functions within the organization. The participating organizations selected SMEs from both civilian and military employees across the services and DISA, excluding contractors. Table 2.3 shows the total number of participants by organization. In total, we held interviews with 125 SMEs. All participants held leadership or supervisor positions, such as director, executive director, and deputy director of an organization or division, as well as lower-level leadership.

SME interviews were conducted by video- or telephone-conference using Microsoft Teams between November 2020 and May 2021. For each interview, one RAND researcher with expertise in military workforce issues led the interview, another study team member with cyber expertise supported by asking clarifying and follow-up questions, and a third study team member took notes. The SME interviews followed a semi-structured interview protocol that we developed and had vetted by action officers (AOs) from each of the organi-

TABLE 2.3
Subject-Matter Expert Interview Participants

Organization	Number of Participants
Marine Corps	14
Army	27
Air Force	17
Navy	22
DISA	45
Total	125

zations comprising the Tri-Chair and the ZBR AO working group members.[2] The SME interview protocol consists of the following five topic areas:

- organizational background and structure
- cybersecurity and IT workforce and workload
- cybersecurity and IT workforce staffing numbers
- potential barriers to efficiency and effectiveness of the cybersecurity and IT work being performed
- potential future changes in cybersecurity and IT workload or requirements.

Not all questions included in the SME interview protocol were asked of every participant. Instead, using input from each organization's representative, we asked each SME a tailored subset of the protocol questions that matched their responsibilities within the organization and their area of expertise. For example, we directed questions that focused on organizational background and structure to the director, executive officer, or deputy director of the organization, while we often asked questions that focused on workload and staffing of lower-level leadership or supervisors within the organization. However, we did provide each SME with the full protocol in advance, and during the interview, they were given an opportunity to respond to any question in the protocol, even if that question was not on their tailored list.

To synthesize the information captured in our SME interview notes, we used a case study approach that produced a summary of findings for each of the participating organizations. Because SME participants answered different questions and because related topics sometimes emerged in responses to different questions, we first used qualitative coding software to organize the information recorded in the SME interview notes according to the five topic areas used in the SME interview protocol. Moreover, we coded the information by organization and position type to facilitate a review of responses within and across those dimensions.

[2] See Appendix A for the SME interview protocol.

After completing the initial coding, we assigned other study team members who did not do any coding to independently review our coding and summarize key findings. We then reviewed the organization-specific summaries and compiled them into a single summary reflecting key findings across all selected organizations.

Work Analysis Data Call

To characterize the work being performed by cybersecurity and IT personnel at the organizations selected to participate in the ZBR, we designed a work analysis data call, which was vetted by AOs from each of the organizations comprising the Tri-Chair and the ZBR AO working group members, to be administered to civilian and military personnel in those positions.[3] The data call took the form of a work analysis questionnaire, which is a common method used by researchers and organizations to understand the nature of the work being performed (Morgeson and Dierdorff, 2011).[4] The data call asked respondents to identify their primary DCWF work role and, if applicable, their secondary DCWF work role, as well as the percentage of their time typically spent in the primary and secondary (if applicable) work role versus time spent performing other work duties. Then, with the respondent's primary work role identified, the data call asked respondents to review the core tasks associated with that DCWF work role and report how *often* they perform those tasks (i.e., task frequency) and how *important* those tasks are to successful performance in the work role (i.e., task importance).[5] Task frequency and importance responses were captured on a 6-point Likert scale corresponding to never (0), yearly (1), monthly (2), weekly (3), daily (4), and hourly (5) for task frequency and a 5-point Likert scale of not important (0), somewhat important (1), important (2), very important (3), and extremely important (4) for task importance. Finally, the data call also asked respondents to comment on whether and how changes to policies, programs, practices, or other features of the work environment would help them perform their current work role more efficiently and effectively.

The data call was programmed into and distributed through an online tool provided by MAX.gov, which provides a "government-wide suite of advanced collaboration, information sharing, data collection, publishing, business intelligence and authentication tools and services used to facilitate cross-government collaboration and knowledge management" (MAX.gov, undated). Responses to the data call were downloaded from MAX.gov to

[3] See Appendix B for the work analysis data call protocol.

[4] The term *work analysis* refers to "the systematic investigation of (a) work role requirements and (b) the broader context within which work roles are enacted" (Morgeson and Dierdorff, 2011, p. 4).

[5] Following guidance from the Tri-Chair, the data call asked respondents about only their primary DCWF work roles (whereas personnel also can have secondary or more work roles) and only the "core" tasks associated with the primary work role (whereas the DCWF also includes "additional" tasks associated with each work role). For more information on core and additional tasks associated with cybersecurity and cyberspace IT work roles, see DoD Cyber Exchange Public, 2020a; and DoD Cyber Exchange Public, 2020b.

RAND computing systems over an encrypted internet connection, and no personal identifiers about respondents were collected.

The data call ran from December 11, 2020, to June 28, 2021. The administration of the data call was staggered for each participating organization, and the number of days that the data call remained open ranged from 27 to 44 days. We received a total of 3,385 responses across all of the selected organizations. After removing incomplete responses and those not associated with personnel from cybersecurity or IT positions, 1,873 responses remained. When compared to a total count of 17,811 civilian and military personnel in the cybersecurity and IT work roles across all of the selected organizations (as reflected in the workforce data and discussed further in Chapter Three), the data call response rate was 11 percent. Counts of responses by pay grade and by work role are shown in Figures 2.1 and 2.2, respectively.[6]

Overall, Figures 2.1 and 2.2 show that the vast majority of data call respondents were civilians in relatively senior pay grades and most respondents performed the cybersecurity role of Information Systems Security Manager (722) and the IT roles of Technical Support Specialist (411), System Administrator (451), and Network Operations Specialist (441).

We used both quantitative and qualitative research methods to analyze data call responses. Most questions lent themselves to simple count analysis and presentation, i.e., task frequency and importance, for which the analysis was conducted at the work role level. For the free-form text responses, e.g., on efficiency and effectiveness, we independently employed both semi-automated and manual thematic coding (Braun and Clarke, 2006; Glaser and Strauss, 1967). For example, word frequency counts provided a simple cue for the subsequent manual review of how these common terms were used in the context of participants' responses. This approach produced a codebook of nine themes (described in more detail below): tools and technology, budget, process, policy, communication, leadership, training, personnel, and the workplace.

Deskside Interviews

To help us further interpret the data call results, we conducted additional work analysis interviews (referred to as *deskside interviews* throughout this report) with staff in specific cybersecurity and IT work roles, focusing on the work roles with the greatest number of responses to the data call. We worked with representatives of each organization to identify participants. Drawing on the representation of organizations across data call respondents, as well as the representation of military and civilian respondents, we determined the number and type of participant to invite to a deskside interview for each work role. We gave preference to staff with more experience in the work role.

[6] Some responses from Figure 2.1 may not be represented in Figure 2.2, because some respondents did not define their primary work role.

FIGURE 2.1
Work Analysis Data Call Responses, by Pay Grade

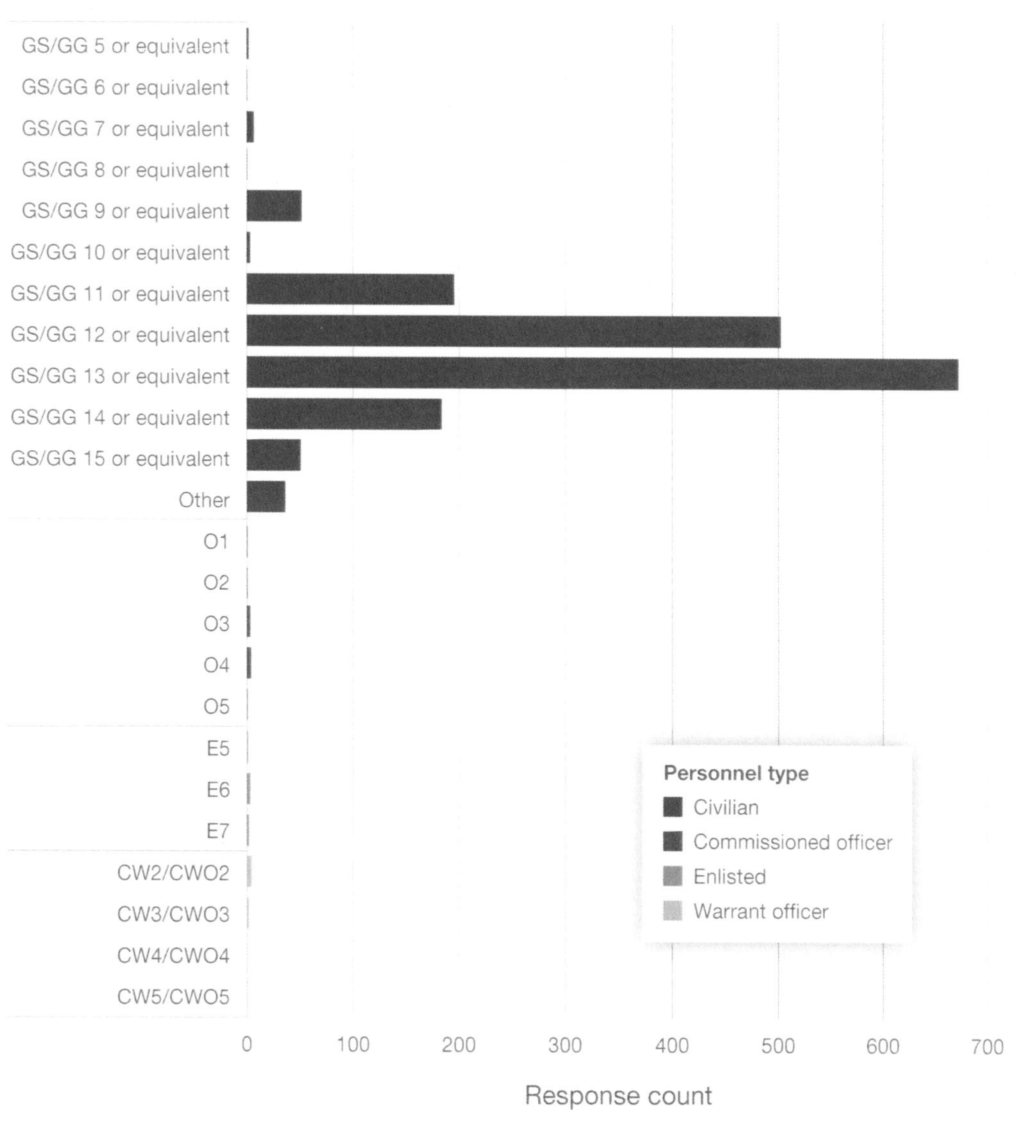

NOTE: CW (Army) or CWO (Navy and Marine Corps) = chief warrant officer; GG = general government; GS = general services.

FIGURE 2.2
Response Count for Cybersecurity and IT Work Roles

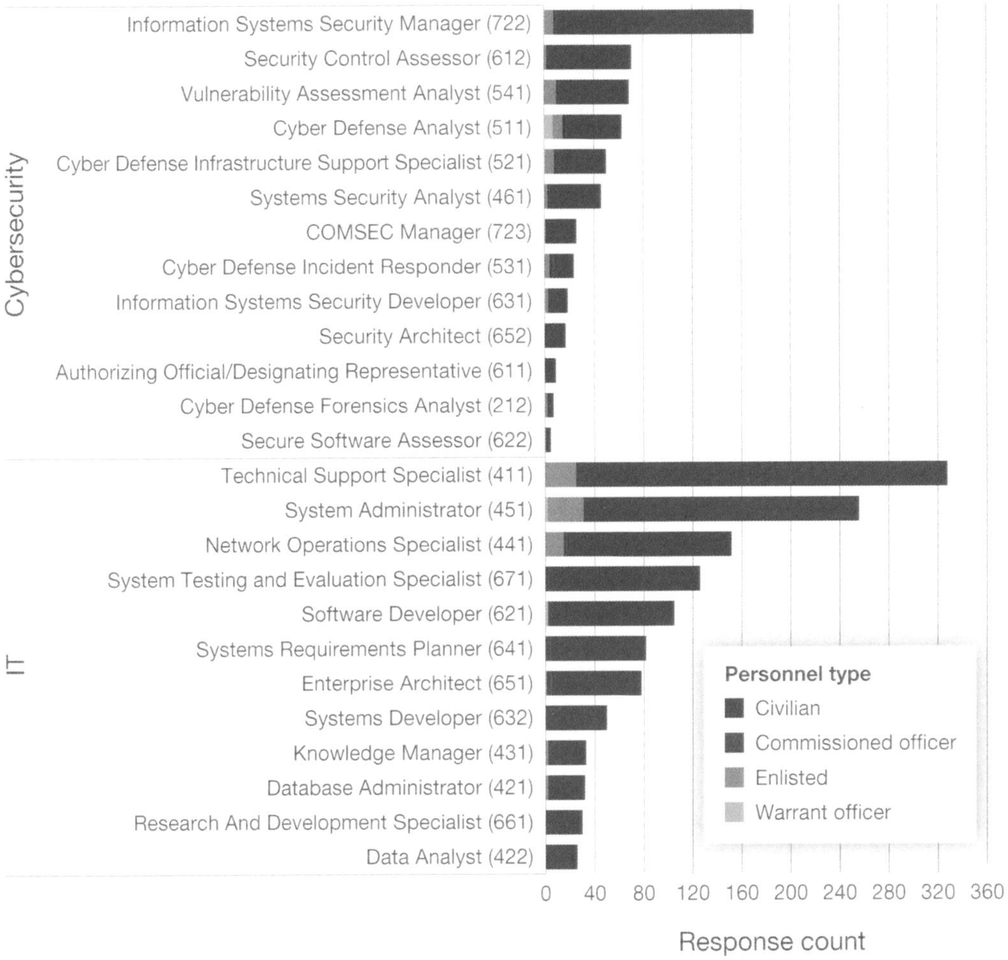

NOTE: Work roles are ordered by response count. DCWF work role numbers are shown in parentheses.

The number of interviews per work role varied across the selected organizations, and the number of work roles from each organization ranged from five to nine, with some overlap. Specifically, we conducted deskside interviews with personnel who performed the Information Systems Security Manager (722), Technical Support Specialist (411), Network Operations Specialist (441), and System Administrator (451) work roles for all selected organizations. Table 2.4 shows the number of participants for each service and DISA, by work role. In total, we held deskside interviews with 87 participants across the selected organizations—25 from the cybersecurity functional area and 62 from the IT functional area.

TABLE 2.4
Number of Deskside Interview Participants, by Work Role

	Number of Deskside Interview Participants					
Work Role	Marine Corps	Army	Air Force	Navy	DISA	Total
Cybersecurity						
Systems Security Analyst (461)				2		2
System Administrator (511)		2				2
Cyber Defense Infrastructure Support Specialist (521)					2	2
Vulnerability Assessment Analyst (541)	2	1				3
Security Control Assessor (612)	1			3		4
Information Systems Security Manager (722)	2	2	3	2	3	12
Cybersecurity participant total	**5**	**5**	**3**	**7**	**5**	**25**
IT						
Technical Support Specialist (411)	2	2	3	2	3	12
Network Operations Specialist (441)	3	2	3	3	2	13
System Administrator (451)	2	2	2	2	3	11
Software Developer (621)		2	3	2		7
Systems Developer (632)		2				2
Systems Requirements Planner (641)				2	4	6
Enterprise Architect (651)		2			3	5
System Testing and Evaluation Specialist (671)				3	3	6
IT participant total	**7**	**12**	**11**	**14**	**18**	**62**
Total participants	12	17	14	21	23	87

Deskside interviews were conducted by video- or telephone-conference using Microsoft Teams between February and July 2021. Similar to the SME interviews, for each interview, one study team member with expertise in military workforce issues led the interview, another study team member with cyber expertise supported by asking clarifying and follow-up questions, and a third study team member took notes. Also, as with the SME interviews, the deskside interviews followed a semi-structured interview protocol that we developed and had vetted by AOs from each of the organizations comprising the Tri-Chair and the ZBR AO working group members.[7]

[7] See Appendix C for the deskside interview protocol.

The deskside interview protocol was designed to assess the extent to which the information collected in the data call aligned with interviewees' own experiences with and understanding of the work role. Following the completion of the data call, the deskside interview protocol was supplemented with information specific to each of the work roles, which summarized the data call responses for task frequency and importance and for efficiency and effectiveness.[8] We asked interviewees to review the information and comment on whether the frequency and importance of the tasks as reported in the data call aligned with their experience in that work role, and if not, why. Also, for tasks in which there was a large variation in reported task frequency and/or importance, we asked interviewees which factors might explain this variation, such as the task being performed more frequently at one organization relative to another. Finally, we asked participants to review and comment on the key themes identified from the data call free-form responses regarding whether and how changes to policies, programs, practices, or other features of the work environment might help them perform their current work role more efficiently and effectively.

In analyzing the data from the deskside interviews, we followed the same procedure that we used for the SME interviews. That is, we first used qualitative coding software to organize the information recorded in the SME interview notes according to the topic areas of the deskside interview protocol. Moreover, we coded the information by organization and position type to facilitate a review of responses within and across those dimensions. After completing the initial coding, we assigned other study team members who did not do any coding to independently review our coded information and to summarize key findings. We then reviewed the organization-specific summaries and compiled them into a single summary reflecting key findings across all selected organizations.

DoD and Private Sector Cyber Workforce Comparison

As shown in Table 2.1, the NDAA asks DoD to compare its cybersecurity and IT manning with comparable industry organizations and consider whether DoD components or subcomponents are under- or over-resourced relative to private sector companies. Direct and specific comparisons between DoD and private industry are difficult to make for many reasons. Here, we describe the limitations and considerations for this kind of analysis, which motivate the data sources used in our analysis. In addition, Appendix D reviews other relevant research on this topic.

First, it is important to understand what motivates the comparison of these two workforces. That is, why are we looking to compare these two groups? Some perceive that private industry has identified a more efficient allocation of such personnel, relative to U.S. government or DoD. However, this perception has yet to be demonstrated objectively or empirically

[8] See Appendix C for an example of the results included in the slide deck specific to each work role.

and likely deserves more consideration to determine when or where appropriate comparisons are possible.

Moreover, when comparing DoD and private sector cyber workforces, we must acknowledge the diversity of the organizations that we wish to compare. The ideal analysis would compare only organizations that are identical along all characteristics relevant to the cyber workforce, such as the organization's mission and size, sophistication of the workforce and IT, management style, etc. Barring that, a second-best approach would be to account for these differences in our analysis; however, the required data to do that are not available. Among the ways that organizations can differ, mission is perhaps the most profound, and we discuss this in detail in Appendix D.

In addition, comparisons between DoD and private sector cyber workforces require a common taxonomy of personnel or, at a minimum, a crosswalk that enables one taxonomy to be translated into another. Although DoD is working to adopt the DCWF for all its cyber work roles, this taxonomy is largely unused by the private sector, which makes comparing the DoD and private sector cyber workforces challenging.

Even if a common taxonomy were used by both groups and we had the data needed to control for differences across organizations, at best we could only compare allocations of personnel across work roles. However, this type of comparison would fall short of evaluating whether one allocation is "better" or "worse," or more or less efficient, than another. To overcome this, data would need to be collected on a relevant cybersecurity or IT outcome, such as time spent addressing help desk calls or the number or impact of cyber incidents. Again, these data were not available for analysis.

Recognizing these limitations, we identified two methods for comparing DoD and private sector cyber workforces. The first method uses Occupational Employment and Wage Statistics data (as of May 2020) from the U.S. Bureau of Labor Statistics (BLS) to compare the composition of *current* staffing between the selected DoD organizations and the private sector. That is, we compared the inventory of private sector workers to the inventory of personnel from the selected DoD organizations participating in the ZBR.

The second method uses job posting data from Burning Glass (a private sector job market analytics company) to compare *unfilled* (gapped) positions between the selected DoD organizations and private industry. For this, we used historical job opening records from April 2020 to March 2021 from Burning Glass to analyze job postings in cybersecurity and IT work roles. Burning Glass has developed a proprietary method for mapping private sector job postings to the NICE Cybersecurity Workforce Framework, a taxonomy of cyber work roles, from which the DCWF is derived (NIST, 2021).[9] These data are made publicly available

[9] NICE work roles were initially specified by Newhouse et al., 2017 and were assigned specific (and mostly unique) knowledge, skills, abilities, and tasks (KSAT). In revision 1 of the NICE framework (Petersen et al., 2020), emphasis was shifted to using task, knowledge, and skill statements as the primary building blocks of a cyber workforce while retaining some adherence to the original work roles defined; these definitions are broken out as separate artifacts and are available at NIST, 2022. During this study, we used Newhouse et al., 2017 as our primary reference because this is the framework on which the DCWF is based.

at CyberSeek.org, which updates the analysis twice a year (CyberSeek, undated). This mapping aligned the KSAT of the NICE framework to "the closest corresponding skills, job titles, job posting keywords, and certifications captured in Burning Glass's database" (Markow and Vilvovsky, 2021).[10] Overall, this mapping provides insight into the distribution of open positions across specialty areas within a variety of private industry categories and an aggregate of 165 public agencies.[11]

Analysis of Civilian Position Descriptions

The selected organizations each provided samples of civilian PDs for work roles within the cybersecurity and IT functional areas. A total of 579 PDs were provided: seven from the selected Marine Corps organizations, 268 from the selected Army organizations, 56 from the selected Air Force organizations, and 124 each from the selected Navy and DISA organizations. Among the PDs provided by each organization, we often found multiple PDs that covered the same position type, with the only difference being the specific billets that each referred to. After removing these duplicates, we were left with a sample of 174 unique PDs.

Each PD lists multiple "main work roles" (which may be different from standard DCWF work roles) followed by an outline of the position's roles, responsibilities, and duties. We compared the sample of civilian PDs to the DCWF cybersecurity and IT work roles, as described by the DCWF master task and knowledge, skills, and abilities list, to assess the extent to which they aligned (Newhouse et al., 2017). We reviewed the main work roles in each PD to determine whether the majority of them collectively matched the description of a DCWF cybersecurity and IT work role. PDs align with the DCWF when a majority of main work roles match those listed in a DCWF work role. Main work roles in PDs are closely related to each other by subject matter and provide a grouping of roles that can be compared with DCWF work roles. Individual tasks might be different across PDs and DCWF work roles, but our comparison relied instead on the collective groupings of main work roles.

We compared the PDs with DCWF work roles, looking for matching keywords and tasks, and in doing so, we coded the PDs as follows:

- *One-to-one match.* Tasks associated with only one PD align with tasks associated with a single DCWF work role.
- *Many-to-one match.* Tasks associated with multiple PDs align with tasks associated with a single DCWF work role.

---

[10] Details of the mapping are not publicly available. Note that a single job posting may align to multiple DCWF work roles.

[11] Public agencies include but are not limited to "the US Government, NSA, Dept of VA, FBI, Dept of Energy, DoD, FAA, DoHS, Army, as well as state and local government agencies" (CompTIA, 2021).

- *One-to-many match.* Tasks associated with only one PD align with tasks associated with multiple DCWF work roles.
- *No match.* Tasks associated with a PD do not align with tasks associated with any DCWF work role.

The purpose of this coding is to provide a high-level look at the extent to which the sample of civilian PDs are compatible with the DCWF. Information like this may be useful to workforce managers as they work to increase alignment and uniformity with the DCWF.

Mapping Data Sources and Methodologies to Themes

Having discussed each element of our research approach in detail, we close this chapter with a summary (in Table 2.5) of how each method and data source maps to and addresses the themes identified by the NDAA requirements.

Together, these methods and data sources represent a repeatable process for performing ZBRs of a cyber (or any other) workforce. In the next chapter, we summarize our findings for each of the five themes, synthesizing the information gathered across all participating organizations, using the methods and data sources and methodologies discussed in this chapter.

TABLE 2.5
Mapping Methods and Data Sources to Themes

	Method or Data Source					
Theme	Analysis of DoD Workforce Data	SME Interviews	Work Analysis Data Call	Deskside Interviews	Comparison of DoD and Private Sector Cyber Workforces	Analysis of Civilian PDs
Current workforce	X					X
Current work performed			X	X		
Manning and capability gaps		X		X	X	
Potential barriers to efficiency and effectiveness		X	X	X		
Potential future changes to work performed or requirements		X		X		

CHAPTER THREE

Findings Across All Selected Organizations

In this chapter, we present our findings by theme, summarizing the information gathered from all selected organizations using the multiple methods and data sources described in Chapter Two. This chapter reflects what we have learned about the cybersecurity and IT workforces at the selected organizations while demonstrating the types of insights that can be produced by this repeatable ZBR process.

Current Workforce

We used DoD workforce data collected during the DoD cyber ZBR effort and our analysis of civilian PDs to characterize the current cybersecurity and IT workforce. We begin this section by summarizing our findings from the workforce data, looking first at the workforce across all cybersecurity and IT work roles and then looking at each functional area in more detail. Following that, we summarize our findings from the PD analysis.

Using the workforce data (i.e., the DoD CIO Workforce Census and organizations' email distribution lists), we find that the selected organizations reported a total of 17,811 cybersecurity and IT personnel, 14,983 (84 percent) of whom are civilians and 2,828 (16 percent) of whom are military personnel.[1] Requirements, personnel, and gaps are shown in Figure 3.1, which is sorted by decreasing requirements. Requirements and personnel are shown as counts on the left-hand axis, while gaps are expressed as percentages on the right-hand axis.

Overall, all organizations reported more requirements than personnel. The selected Army organizations reported the greatest number of requirements and personnel, followed by selected organizations from the Air Force, Navy, DISA, and Marine Corps. Overall, we find no strong correlation between total number of requirements or personnel and the gap (i.e., work roles with more requirements or personnel do not consistently have larger gaps). For example, while the Army and Air Force organizations reported the highest number of requirements and personnel, the Navy and Marine Corps organizations reported the largest gaps (33 percent and 30 percent respectively). And although DISA reported the fourth-lowest

[1] Contractors are not included in the DCWF; instead, they are binned by type of work performed per the DoDM 8570.01, 2015. As a result, contractors do not appear in our counts of personnel by DCWF work role or functional area.

FIGURE 3.1
Total Civilian and Military Cybersecurity and IT Requirements, Personnel, and Gaps for Selected Organizations

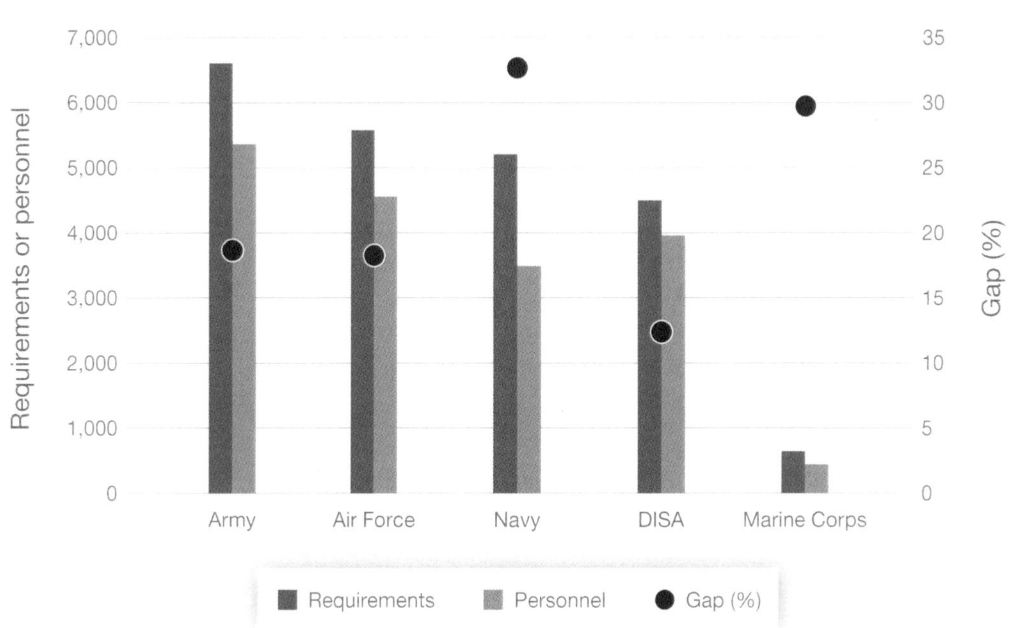

number of requirements, it also reported the lowest gap (12 percent), followed by the Air Force (18 percent) and Army (19 percent).

Next, we look at the data separately for the civilian and military workforces, by service, first for the cybersecurity functional area and then for the IT functional area.

Cybersecurity

Figure 3.2 shows the total number of civilian and military personnel, requirements, and gaps in the cybersecurity work roles for the selected organizations, by selected organization and sorted by decreasing requirements. The upper panel shows civilian results, while the lower panel shows military results.

Overall, the selected organizations reported 2,978 cybersecurity personnel: 2,723 (91 percent) of whom are civilians, while 255 (9 percent) are military personnel. Note, the selected Army organizations did not provide military requirements or personnel data for the cybersecurity functional area and are therefore not displayed in the lower panel of Figure 3.2.

The upper panel of Figure 3.2 shows that although the Army organizations reported the largest number of civilian cybersecurity personnel, they also reported a modest personnel gap of 24 percent. Furthermore, the DISA, Air Force, and Navy organizations each have similar levels of requirements, but different gaps. For example, the DISA organizations show the lowest gap at just 7 percent, while the Air Force and Navy organizations show gaps of 23 per-

FIGURE 3.2

Civilian and Military Cybersecurity Requirements, Personnel, and Gaps for Selected Organizations

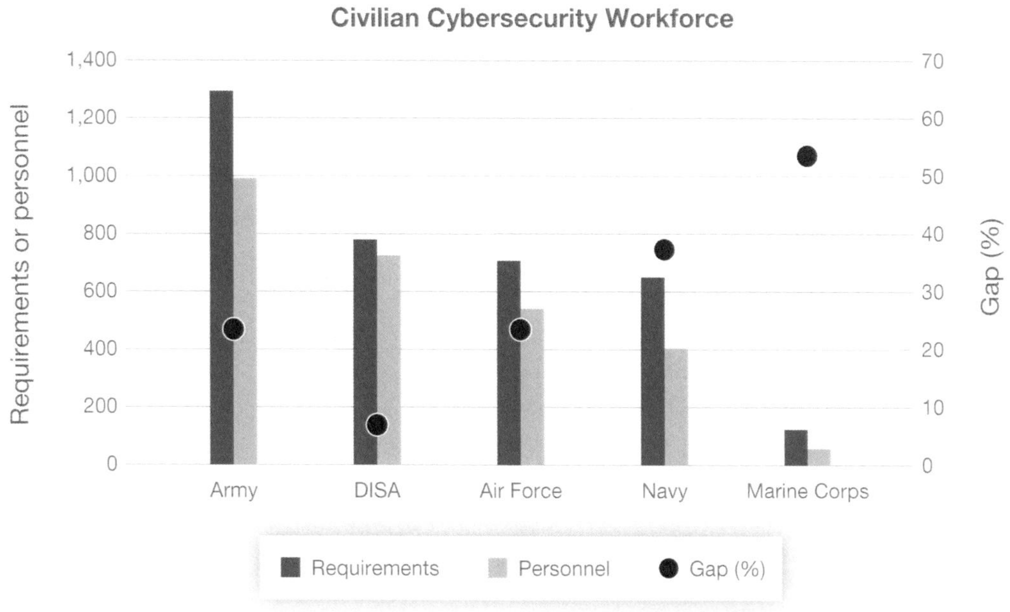

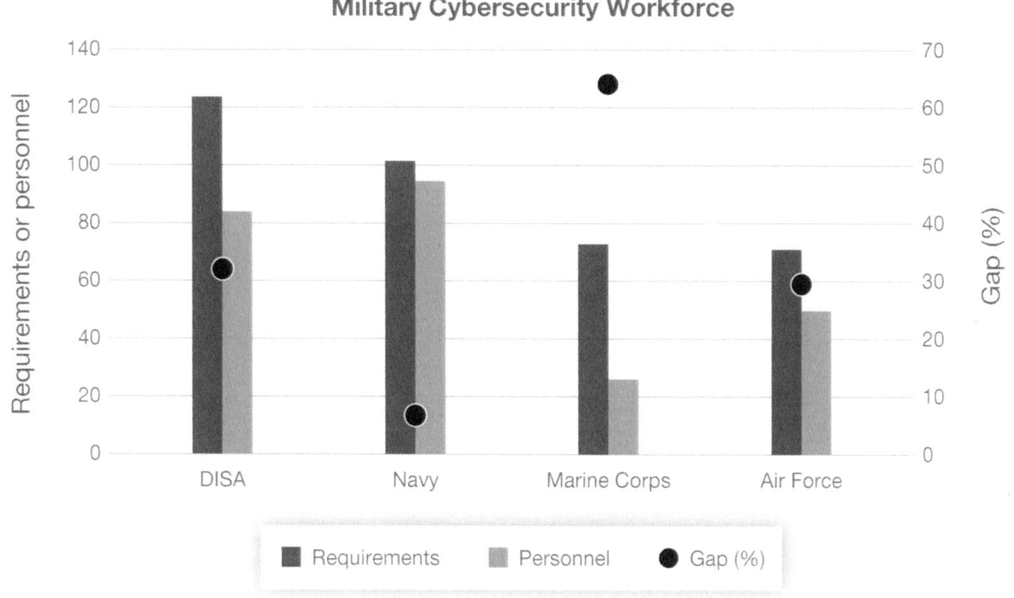

NOTE: The selected Army organizations did not provide military requirements or personnel data for the cybersecurity functional area.

cent and 38 percent, respectively. Finally, the Marine Corps organizations show the highest gap at 54 percent with requirements of just 121 personnel.

Examining the military data (lower panel of Figure 3.2), we see that both the DISA and Navy organizations reported similar military personnel requirements (124 and 102, respectively), but they have dramatically different gaps: Navy organizations show a 7-percent gap and the DISA organizations show a 32-percent gap. Both the Marine Corps and Air Force organizations reported similar requirements of slightly more than 70 personnel, yet the Marine Corps organizations show the highest gap at 64 percent while the Air Force organizations show a 30-percent gap.

Next, we break out the data on personnel, requirements, and gaps by DCWF work role for the cybersecurity functional area, aggregating all organizations' reported data. Figures 3.3 and 3.4 show the civilian and military results, respectively, by descending requirements.

As Figure 3.3 shows, civilian cybersecurity personnel across the selected organizations are mostly performing in core functional roles, such as Information Systems Security Manager (722), Cyber Defense Analyst (511), and Vulnerability Assessment Analysis (541). Most work roles show a gap between 15 percent and 30 percent, with an overall average gap of

FIGURE 3.3

Civilian Cybersecurity Requirements, Personnel, and Gaps for Selected Organizations, by DCWF Work Role

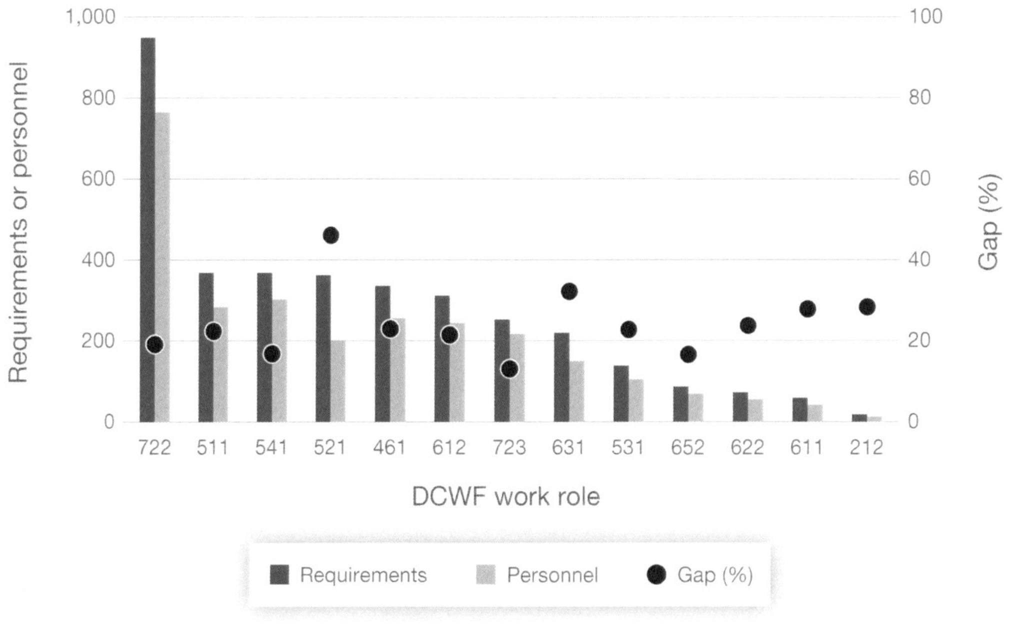

NOTE: DCWF work role numbers correspond to the following roles: 722 = Information Systems Security Manager; 511 = Cyber Defense Analyst; 541 = Vulnerability Assessment Analyst; 521 = Cyber Defense Infrastructure Support Specialist; 461 = Systems Security Analyst; 612 = Security Control Assessor; 723 = COMSEC Manager; 631 = Information Systems Security Developer; 531 = Cyber Defense Incident Responder; 652 = Security Analyst; 622 = Secure Software Assessor; 611 = Authorizing Official/Designating Representative; 212 = Cyber Defense Forensics Analyst.

24 percent.[2] COMSEC Manager (723) has the smallest gap (13 percent), while the Cyber Defense Infrastructure Support (521) has the largest gap (46 percent). As with overall cybersecurity and IT personnel gaps, gaps for specific work roles do not appear to be strongly correlated with the number of civilian requirements or personnel.

Figure 3.4 shows personnel, requirements, and gaps for military cybersecurity work roles. Again, note that these data do not include the selected Army organizations because military requirements and personnel data were not available by work role. Also note that there are no requirements or personnel for the Security Control Assessor (612) and Secure Software Assessor (622) roles. Overall, we find a lot fewer military cybersecurity personnel and requirements compared with civilian cybersecurity personnel and requirements. As a result, even small differences between personnel and requirements produce large gaps.

Military cybersecurity personnel at the selected organizations are mostly performing Systems Security Analyst (461), Information Systems Security Manager (722), and Cyber Defense

FIGURE 3.4

Military Cybersecurity Requirements, Personnel, and Gaps for Selected Organizations, by DCWF Work Role

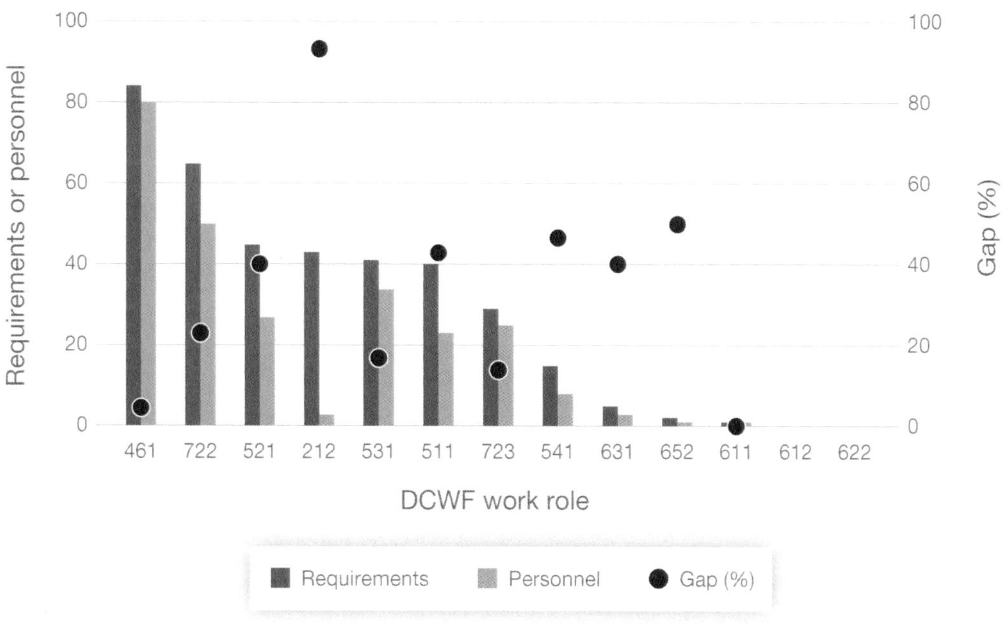

NOTE: Army data were not available. There are no personnel or requirements for the Security Control Assessor (612) and Secure Software Assessor (622) work roles. DCWF work role numbers correspond to the following roles: 461 = Systems Security Analyst; 722 = Information Systems Security Manager; 521 = Cyber Defense Infrastructure Support Specialist; 212 = Cyber Defense Forensics Analyst; 531 = Cyber Defense Incident Responder; 511 = Cyber Defense Analyst; 723 = COMSEC Manager; 541 = Vulnerability Assessment Analyst; 631 = Information Systems Security Developer; 652 = Security Analyst; 611 = Authorizing Official/Designating Representative; 612 = Security Control Assessor; 622 = Secure Software Assessor.

[2] We computed this average by dividing the sum of requirements by the sum of personnel.

Incident Responder (531) roles. Moreover, based on these data, these military cybersecurity positions are gapped at a higher percentage on average relative to civilian cybersecurity roles (31 percent versus 24 percent); most military work roles show gaps between 20 percent and 50 percent. The Cyber Defense Forensics Analyst (212) has the highest gap at 93 percent. And, even though Systems Security Analyst (461) is the most common military work role at the selected organizations, it has one of the smallest gaps (5 percent), along with Authorizing Official/Designating Representative (611), which has no gap. Furthermore, we again see no relationship between the number of requirements or personnel and the size of the gap by work role.

Information Technology

Figure 3.5 shows the total number of civilian and military personnel, requirements, and gaps in IT work roles for the selected organizations, by service and sorted by decreasing requirements. The upper panel shows civilian results, while the lower panel shows military results.

Overall, the selected organizations reported 13,658 IT personnel: 12,260 (90 percent) of whom are civilians, while 1,398 (10 percent) are military personnel. Note, the selected Army organizations did not provide military requirements or personnel data for the IT functional area and are therefore not displayed in the lower panel of Figure 3.5. The upper panel of Figure 3.5 shows that all selected organizations, with the exception of the Marine Corps organizations, were of roughly equal size, reporting civilian personnel and requirement values between approximately 3,000 and 4,000. However, we do see some variation in gaps: The Navy organizations reported the largest gap of 33 percent, and the DISA organizations reported the lowest gap of 7 percent. We also note that, except for the Marine Corps organizations, the size of the gap decreases with the number of requirements.

Examining the military data (lower panel of Figure 3.5), both the DISA and Air Force organizations reported similar military requirements (780 and 735, respectively), while the Marine Corps and Navy organizations reported much lower requirements of 269 and 168, respectively. As was the case for the civilian IT work roles, the size of the gap decreases with the number of requirements. The DISA organizations reported the largest gap (34 percent), while the Navy organizations reported the lowest gap (18 percent).

Next, Figures 3.6 and 3.7 show personnel, requirements, and gaps by DCWF work role for the IT functional area. As we did for the cybersecurity functional area, we have aggregated all organizations' reported data and sorted results by descending requirements.

As Figure 3.6 shows, civilian IT personnel are mostly performing foundational IT roles, such as Technical Support Specialist (411), System Administrator (451), and Network Operations Specialist (441). Most work roles show a gap of between 15 percent and 25 percent, with an overall average of 19 percent. Research and Development Specialist (661) shows the largest gap (35 percent), whereas Data Analyst (422) shows the smallest gap (10 percent). As before, gaps do not appear to be strongly correlated with the number of civilian requirements or personnel.

FIGURE 3.5
Civilian and Military IT Requirements, Personnel, and Gaps for Selected Organizations

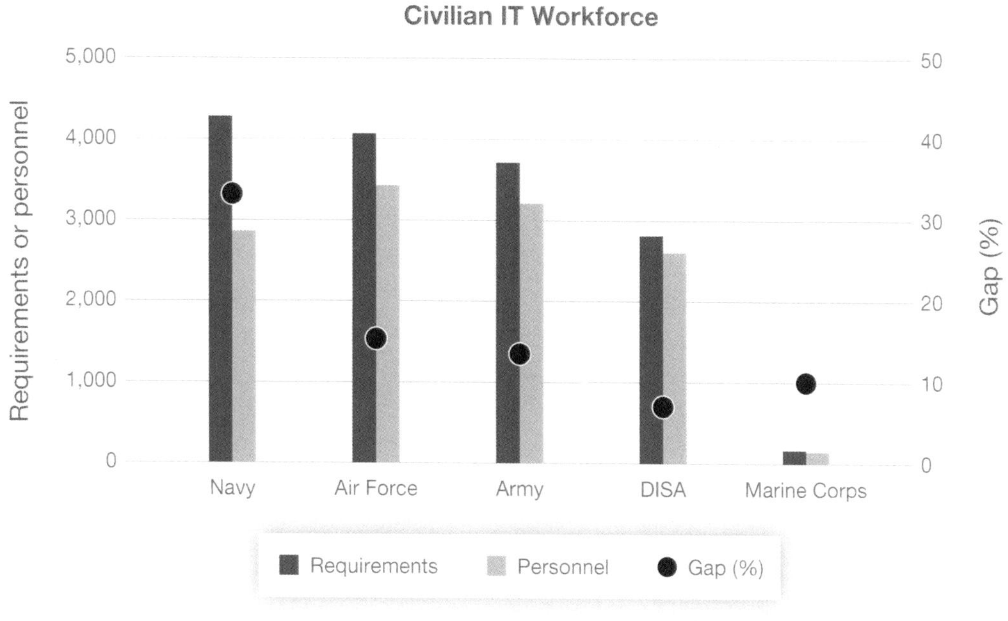

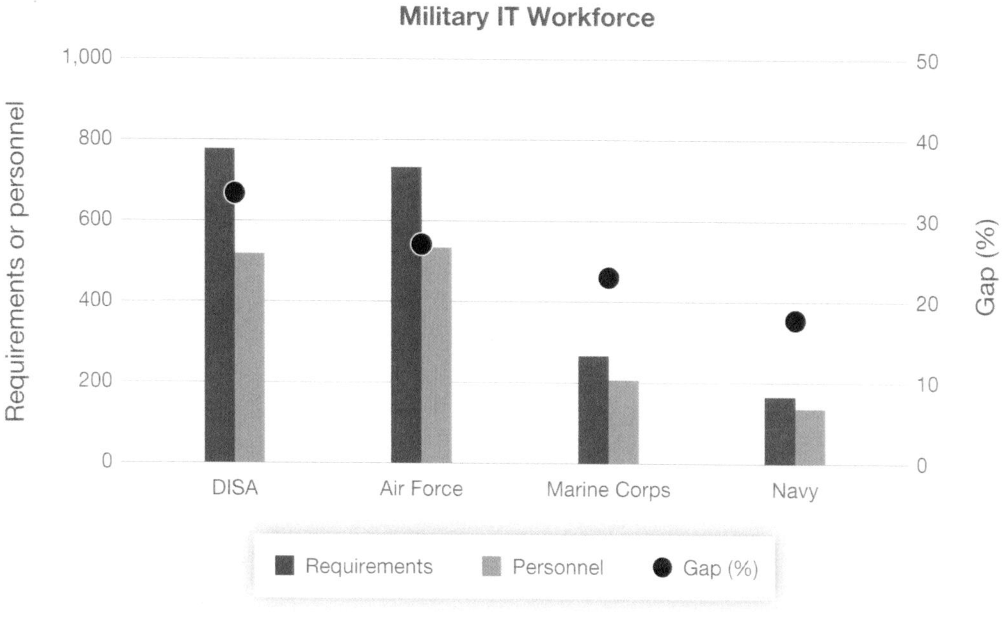

NOTE: The selected Army organizations did not provide military requirements or personnel data for the IT functional area.

FIGURE 3.6

Civilian IT Requirements, Personnel, and Gaps for Selected Organizations, by DCWF Work Role

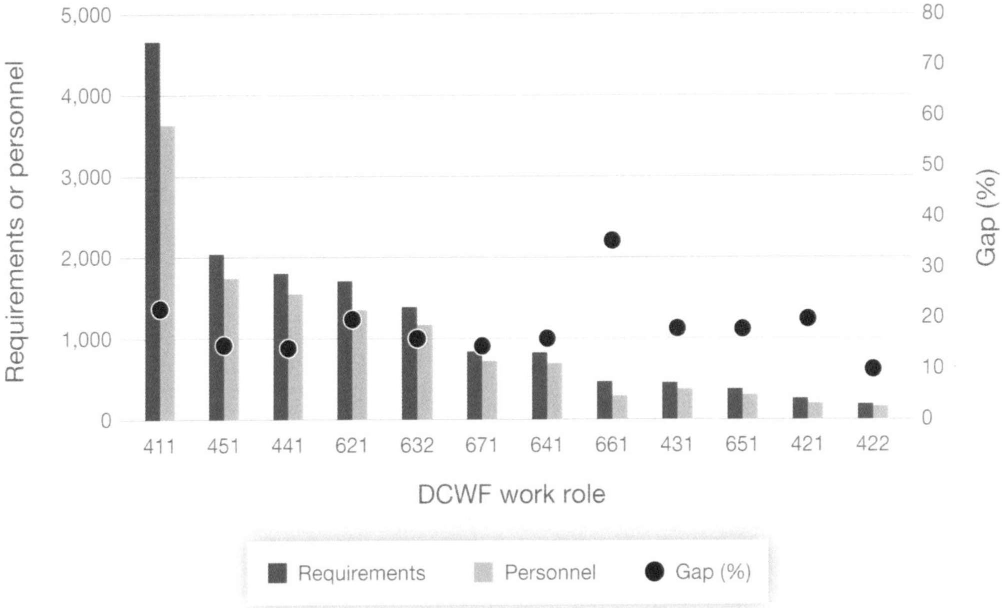

NOTE: DCWF work role numbers correspond to the following roles: 411 = Technical Support Specialist; 451 = System Administrator; 441 = Network Operations Specialist; 621 = Software Developer; 632 = Systems Developer; 671 = System Testing and Evaluation Specialist; 641 = Systems Requirements Planner; 661 = Research and Development Specialist; 431 = Knowledge Manager; 651 = Enterprise Architect; 421 = Database Administrator; 422 = Data Analyst.

Figure 3.7 shows personnel, requirements, and gaps for military IT work roles. Again, note that these data do not include the selected Army organizations because military requirements and personnel data were not available by work role.

As was the case for the cybersecurity work roles, there are many fewer military IT personnel compared with civilian IT personnel and requirements (although, still many more personnel relative to military *cybersecurity* personnel), and so, small differences between personnel and requirements will produce large gaps. Similar to civilian IT personnel, military IT personnel are mostly performing foundational IT roles, such as Technical Support Specialist (411), System Administrator (451), and Network Operations Specialist (441). Also, the military IT positions—like the military cybersecurity positions—are gapped at a higher percentage relative to civilian IT roles: Most roles show gaps of between 20 percent and 50 percent. Systems Requirements Planner (641) and Software Developer (621) have the largest gaps at 68 percent and 60 percent, respectively. Even though Technical Support Specialist (411) is the most common military IT work role at the selected organizations, it also has one of the smallest gaps (18 percent), along with Research and Development Specialist (661), which is gapped at 14 percent. Enterprise Architect (651) is the only work role that is overmanned, with five

FIGURE 3.7
Military IT Requirements, Personnel, and Gaps for Selected Organizations, by DCWF Work Role

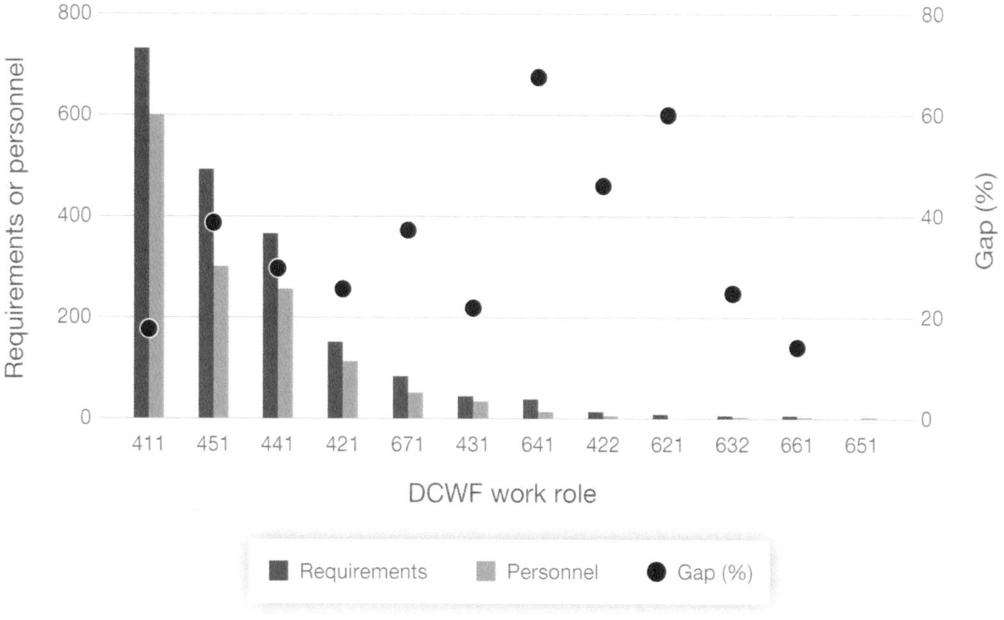

NOTE: Army military IT requirements and personnel data were not available by work role. DCWF work role numbers correspond to the following roles: 411 = Technical Support Specialist; 451 = System Administrator; 441 = Network Operations Specialist; 421 = Database Administrator; 671 = System Testing and Evaluation Specialist; 431 = Knowledge Manager; 641 = Systems Requirements Planner; 422 = Data Analyst; 621 = Software Developer; 632 = Systems Developer; 661 = Research and Development Specialist; 651 = Enterprise Architect.

personnel for three requirements. Overall, we again see no relationship between the number of requirements or personnel and the size of the gap.

Examination of Position Descriptions

As described in Chapter Two, we also analyzed a sample of civilian cybersecurity and IT PDs provided by the selected organizations to assess the extent to which they align with the KSAT found in DCWF work roles. We grouped PDs into four categories based on our assessment of their match to DCWF work roles: a one-to-one match, a many-to-one match, a one-to-many match, and no match. Figure 3.8 summarizes the results.

Of the 174 PDs that we examined, nearly one-half (45 percent, 78) matched many to one, meaning that the tasks contained in multiple PDs align with tasks associated with a single DCWF work role. For example, tasks in multiple IT specialist PDs mapped to the Cyber Defense Analyst (511) work role. Moreover, tasks in multiple PDs aligned with the Technical Support Specialist (411) work role, which is unsurprising given the generalist nature of that work role. About one-fifth (21 percent, 37) of the PDs matched one to many, meaning that

FIGURE 3.8
Matching Civilian PDs with Cybersecurity and IT DCWF Work Roles

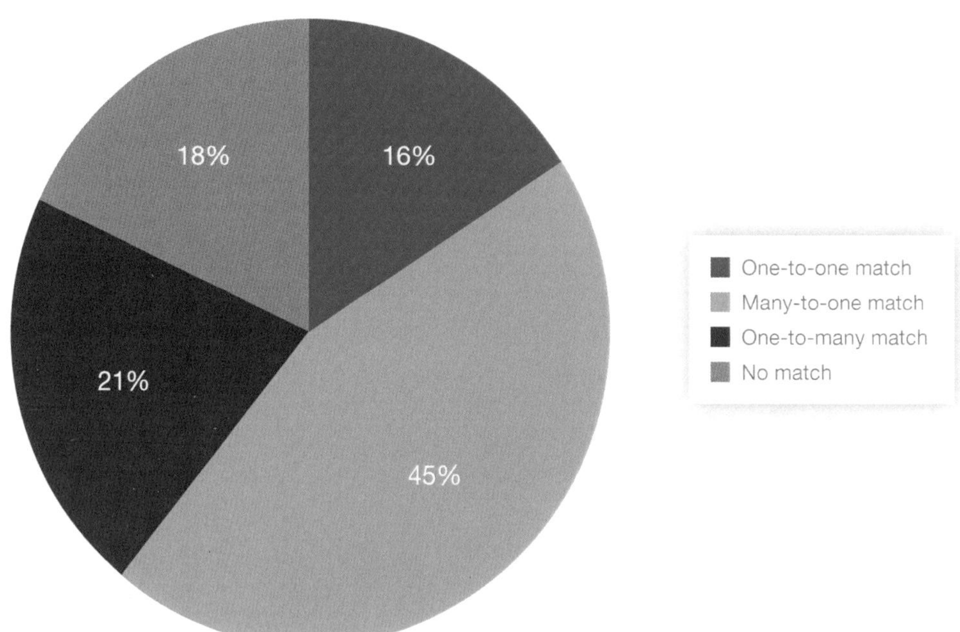

the tasks contained in a single PD align with the tasks associated with multiple DCWF work roles. For example, a computer engineer PD matches to the Software Developer (621) and Systems Developer (632) work roles, a data administrator PD matches to the Database Administrator (421) and System Administrator (451) work roles, and a data analyst PD matches to the Knowledge Manager (431) and Research and Development Specialist (661) work roles. Another 16 percent (28) of the PDs matched one to one, meaning that the tasks contained in a single PD align with the tasks associated with a single DCWF work role. For example, the computer scientist PD and the Software Developer (621) work role match only to one another, and the same is true for the program analyst PD and the Cyber Policy and Strategy Planner (752) work role.

Finally, 18 percent (31) of the PDs that we reviewed do not match any of the DCWF cybersecurity or IT work roles. These include PDs for supervisory roles, which tend to be diverse and position specific. Others are PDs for trainee positions that may be filled by interns or students. Other PDs that do not match a DCWF cybersecurity or IT work role are of a very technical nature that are specific to a particular organization, such as a cyber operations planner PD, or are more administrative, such as an administrative specialist PD.

Current Work Performed

To characterize the type of cybersecurity and IT work currently being performed across the selected organizations, we turn to information collected in the work analysis data call in which respondents were asked about the frequency and importance of DCWF tasks performed as part of their primary cybersecurity or IT work role.

Insights from this analysis may be useful to leadership who oversee the execution of the DCWF, as well as to members of the DoD cyber workforce and their managers. For *leadership*, the work role–level results could shed light on whether personnel are engaging in core DCWF tasks at the frequency and with the self-reported importance that would be expected, given their assessment of the work role's contributions to the larger cyber mission. For the *workforce* and their *managers*, the task-level results could highlight whether the workforce is performing core DCWF tasks and assigning the same level of importance as required for their organization's cyber workforce management plan. For these reasons, we present both the role- and task-level results for task frequency and importance.

Here, we focus on the 14 cybersecurity and IT work roles that were featured in the five unpublished RAND reports that we provided to the participating organizations—one report for each DoD service plus DISA—during the execution of the DoD cyber ZBR. These 14 work roles were originally selected on the basis of each having a sufficient number of data call responses to enable some measure of generalization.[3] Among these 14 work roles, five are cybersecurity:

- Systems Security Analyst (461)
- Cyber Defense Infrastructure Support Specialist (521)
- Vulnerability Assessment Analyst (541)
- Security Control Assessor (612)
- Information Systems Security Manager (722)

and nine are IT:

- Technical Support Specialist (411)
- Database Administrator (421)
- Network Operations Specialist (441)
- System Administrator (451)
- Software Developer (621)
- Systems Developer (632)
- Systems Requirements Planner (641)
- Enterprise Architect (651)
- System Testing and Evaluation Specialist (671).

[3] Because of a data collection error, data call results for Cyber Defense Analyst (511) do not include information on task importance, so they have been excluded from these results.

Figures 3.9 and 3.10 depict the distribution of task frequency and importance values, as reported by data call respondents, for each of the 14 work roles. Task frequency is shown in purple in Figure 3.9 along with the median percentage of time that the respondents reported spending in their primary work role; task importance is shown in green in Figure 3.10. The results are displayed using box plots, which show that while most work roles have a broad range of frequency and importance values, most of the responses were more tightly clustered around moderate frequency and high-importance values. In the two figures, the yellow lines denote the median reported task frequency and importance values. The boxes depict the middle 50 percent of responses and the vertical lines extending from these boxes (*whiskers*) show the full range of responses received, from the minimum value to the maximum value.

The distribution of task frequency and importance responses shown by the whiskers is broad—at least one respondent in almost all work roles stated that they perform a task hourly

FIGURE 3.9

Distribution of Task Frequency Responses and Median Time Spent in the Primary Work Role for the 14 Featured Cybersecurity and IT Work Roles

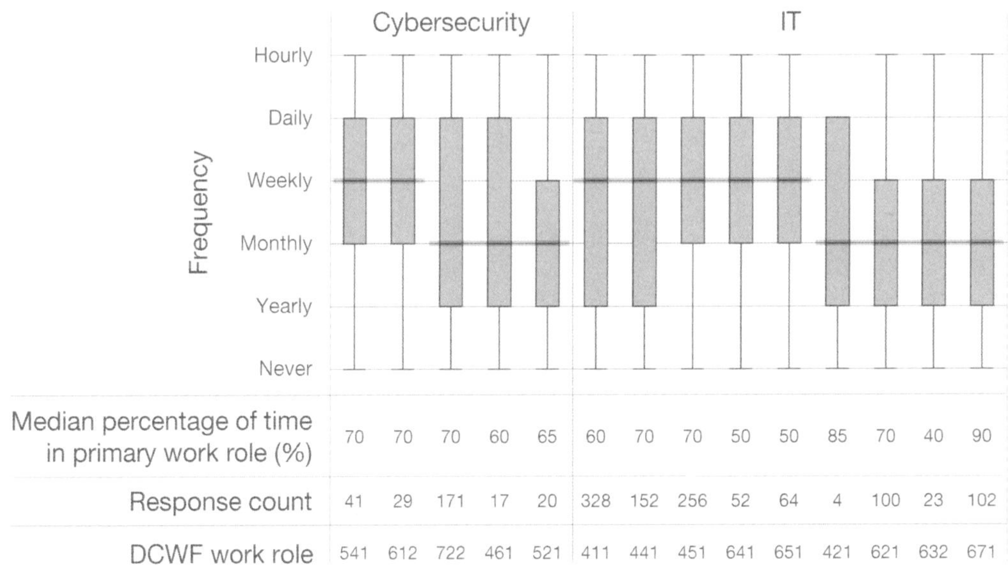

NOTE: This figure shows the distribution of task frequency responses and the median percentage of time respondents reported spending in their primary work roles. Respondents were asked to estimate the time spent in their primary work roles in increments of ten percentage points. The box plot depicts the median value (yellow lines) of reported task frequency for a given work role. The boxes depict the middle 50 percent of responses, and the whiskers range from the maximum to the minimum response values. Work roles are sorted by decreasing median of frequency value, then by decreasing range of middle 50 percent of responses. DCWF work role numbers correspond to the following roles: 541 = Vulnerability Assessment Analyst; 612 = Security Control Assessor; 722 = Information Systems Security Manager; 461 = Systems Security Analyst; 521 = Cyber Defense Infrastructure Support Specialist; 411 = Technical Support Specialist; 441 = Network Operations Specialist; 451 = System Administrator; 641 = Systems Requirements Planner; 651 = Enterprise Architect; 421 = Database Administrator; 621 = Software Developer; 632 = Systems Developer; 671 = System Testing and Evaluation Specialist.

FIGURE 3.10
Distribution of Task Importance Responses for the 14 Featured Cybersecurity and IT Work Roles

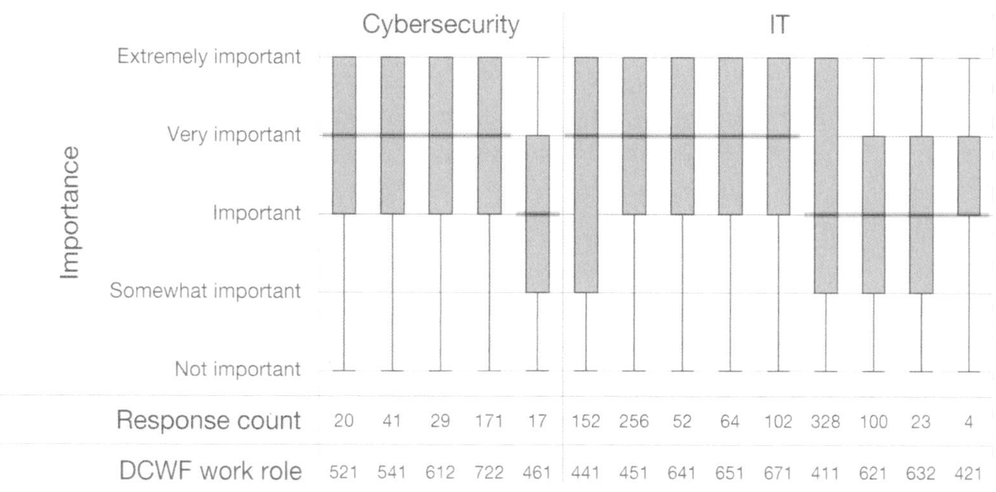

NOTE: The box plot depicts the median value (yellow lines) of reported task importance for a given work role. The boxes depict the middle 50 percent of responses, and the whiskers range from the maximum to the minimum response values. Work roles are sorted by decreasing median of importance value, then by decreasing range of middle 50 percent of responses. DCWF work role numbers correspond to the following roles: 521 = Cyber Defense Infrastructure Support Specialist; 541 = Vulnerability Assessment Analyst; 612 = Security Control Assessor; 722 = Information Systems Security Manager; 461 = Systems Security Analyst; 441 = Network Operations Specialist; 451 = System Administrator; 641 = Systems Requirements Planner; 651 = Enterprise Architect; 671 = System Testing and Evaluation Specialist; 411 = Technical Support Specialist; 621 = Software Developer; 632 = Systems Developer; 421 = Database Administrator.

or never and that their tasks were extremely or not important. We note that these broad distributions in frequency and importance results could have two potential explanations that cannot be distinguished in the data: (1) respondents' opinions varied within tasks (i.e., different people rated the same tasks very differently) and/or (2) respondents' opinions varied across different tasks (i.e., a respondent rated two tasks very differently).

Figures 3.9 and 3.10 show that the median *frequency* with which personnel reported conducting tasks (from yearly to weekly) is more varied than *importance* values across the work roles. In general, respondents perceived their tasks to be at least important; the distribution of responses skews toward greater importance values. Overall, median task frequency and importance values are similar for the cybersecurity and IT work roles. Furthermore, looking at the distribution of responses within a work role, we see that perceptions of the frequency and importance of tasks conducted vary substantially.[4] Although subsequent figures in this section focus on the *median* values of task frequency and importance as a way to summarize

[4] Note that although respondents were asked how often they conduct particular tasks (i.e., frequency), they were not asked how much time they spend on the task each time they perform it (i.e., duration), as would

the findings, the data presented in Figures 3.9 and 3.10 show that there is important variation around the median: Respondents within the same work role do not share a single opinion on the frequency and importance of the tasks that they conduct.

Moreover, respondents' perceptions of task frequency and importance should be considered alongside the percentage of time that they spend on their primary work role, which was also collected in the data call and reported in Figure 3.9. For example, Systems Developers (632) reported a median task frequency of "monthly," but they reportedly spend only 40 percent of their time on tasks related to their primary work role. On the other hand, System Administrators (451) reported spending 70 percent of their time on their primary work role and performing tasks with a median frequency of "weekly."

Next, at the work role–level, we examine the relationship between perceived task frequency and importance. To aid in the interpretation of the data call results, we conceptualized this relationship with a four-quadrant matrix, as shown in Figure 3.11.

The top-left quadrant of Figure 3.11 reflects tasks that are highly important, but performed relatively infrequently (i.e., yearly or monthly). These tasks may be more strategic

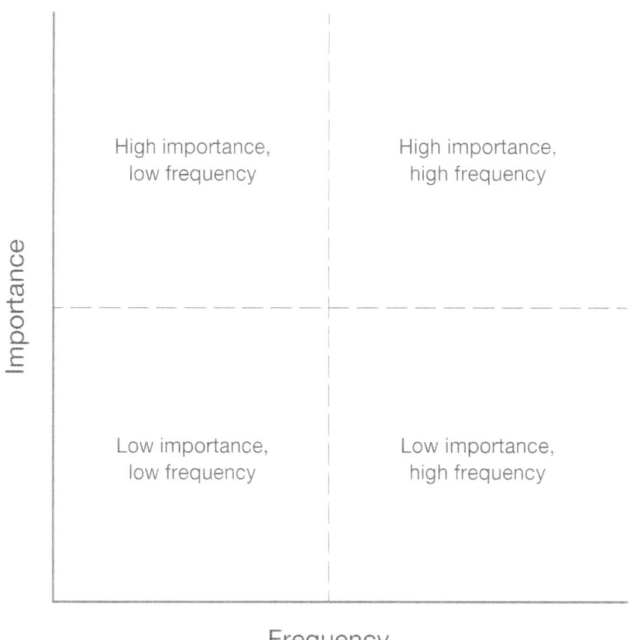

be done in a work diary study. Therefore, the information collected in our work analysis data call could not reveal whether a task that is conducted yearly also takes months to complete, for example.

in that they may be vital to the organization's ability to meet the cyber mission but are only performed episodically, or are event driven. Examples might include strategic planning or replacing and maintaining critical cyber infrastructure. Tasks that would fall in the top-right quadrant, on the other hand, are both highly important and frequently performed (i.e., daily or hourly). These tasks could be considered tactical and may be highly repetitive (e.g., call center support). Because of the high importance and high frequency of these tasks, managers may consider reviewing them for overwork and capacity issues. However, burnout and attrition may be the result of several factors related to the work environment. To determine if highly frequent tasks are associated with burnout and attrition, managers should assess which other job demands are placed on personnel who perform them, which could lead to sentiments of burnout and attrition (Alarcon, 2011).

Tasks that would fall to the bottom-right quadrant, having low importance and high frequency, may not be critical to the organization's success, and yet, they may consume a great deal of staff time. These tasks may be candidates for automation; the high frequency could translate into a greater reward for automating these tasks (i.e., freeing up considerable labor hours) while their low importance reduces the risk that might come about with minimizing or eliminating the role of humans in performing these tasks. Finally, tasks in the bottom-left quadrant would be of both low importance and low frequency. These tasks also could be candidates for automation; however, the low frequency with which these tasks are performed reduces the potential benefit of investing in automation to perform them. Personnel who perform low-frequency tasks (whether of high or low importance) may experience some amount of perishability of skills (though it depends of course on the task). Thus, leadership might consider supporting refresher training programs for such tasks.

We next plot data call results on the conceptual matrix described above. Whereas Figures 3.9 and 3.10 showed the distribution of respondents' perceptions of task frequency and importance by work role, Figures 3.12 and 3.13 show the median task frequency and importance values across all tasks for the five featured cybersecurity work roles and the nine featured IT work roles, respectively. These figures seek to broadly characterize perceptions of cybersecurity and IT tasks. In both figures, the size of the shape reflects the number of tasks that had the same median value for frequency and importance: In other words, a bigger shape signifies more tasks with those reported median values, while a smaller shape signifies fewer reported tasks with those reported median values.

As Figures 3.12 and 3.13 show, most tasks are clustered in the top two quadrants, with median values of high importance but with more-varied frequency. We find a weak correlation (R^2 of 0.43 and 0.42, respectively) between task frequency and importance, meaning that tasks that were rated as more frequent generally were also more likely to be rated as more important. Comparing across the cybersecurity and IT functional areas, we note that none of

FIGURE 3.12
Median Task Frequency and Importance for All Tasks for the Five Featured Cybersecurity Work Roles Across All Selected Organizations

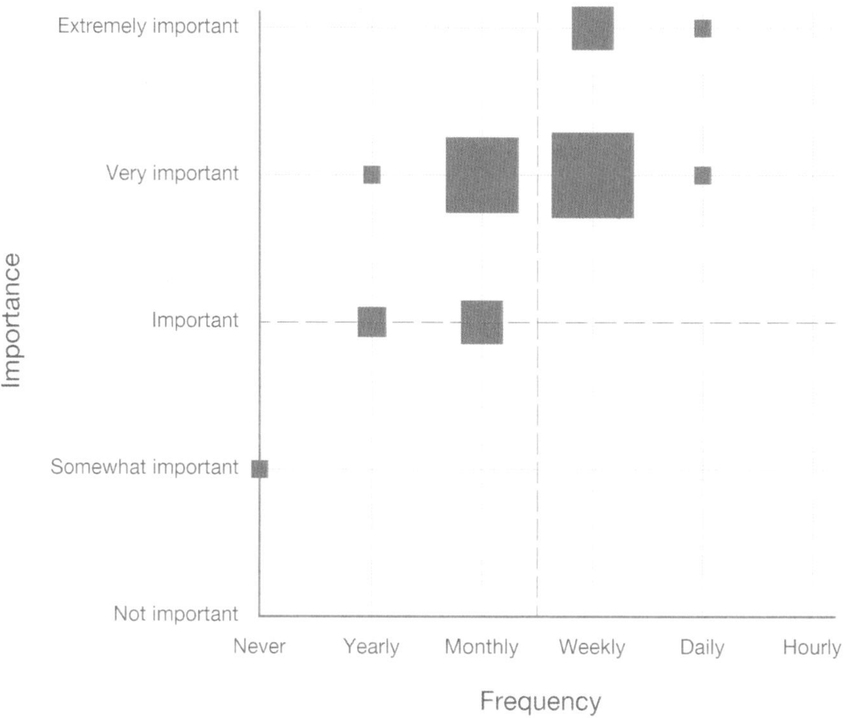

NOTE: The size of the square corresponds to the number of tasks with the same median frequency and importance values.

the IT tasks received median ratings lower than important, whereas that was not the case for a few cybersecurity tasks. Such tasks could be candidates for automation. For tasks that were reported as being performed less frequently, refresher training may be warranted if the skills required to perform these tasks decay when not in use. Additionally, four IT tasks were rated as important but never performed, on average, which may reflect a staffing shortage.

Next, in Figures 3.14–3.17, we show median task frequency and importance values for specific DCWF work roles. Among the 14 work roles summarized in Figures 3.9 and 3.10, we narrow the focus to the four DCWF work roles that were featured in more-detailed organization-level analyses shared directly with the services and DISA.[5] These four work roles include one cybersecurity work role—Information Systems Security Manager (722, Figure 3.14)—and three IT work roles—Technical Support Specialist (411, Figure 3.15), Network Operations Specialist (441, Figure 3.16), and System Administrator (451, Figure 3.17). In the DCWF, tasks are referred to as KSATs, which are denoted in the following figures by

[5] Results for the remaining ten DCWF work roles are shown in Appendix E.

FIGURE 3.13
Median Task Frequency and Importance for All Tasks for the Nine Featured IT Work Roles Across All Selected Organizations

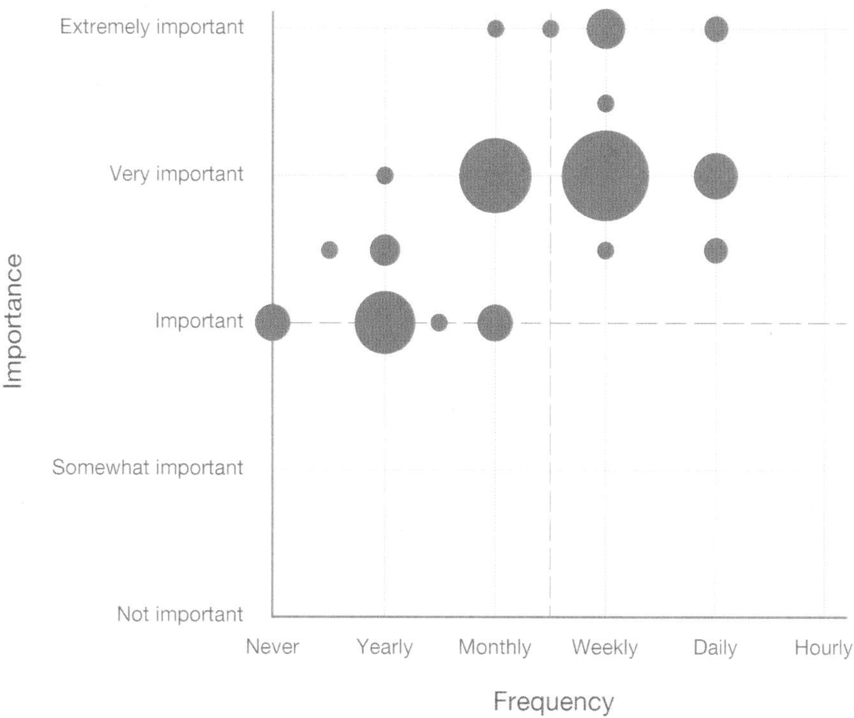

NOTE: The size of the circle corresponds to the number of tasks with the same median frequency and importance values.

three- or four-digit codes.[6] Additionally, many tasks have the same median values for task frequency and importance; therefore, one dot in a figure may be labeled with multiple KSAT codes. We note that there is variation among the selected organizations, and although that level of detail is not shown in these figures, we did provide more detailed information directly to the services and DISA.

Consistent with the work role–level results shown in Figures 3.9 and 3.10 and the task-level results shown for all cybersecurity work roles in Figure 3.12, the task-level results for Information Systems Security Manager (722) in Figure 3.14 show that all tasks were perceived, on average, as important to extremely important, across all selected organizations, with almost 90 percent of the tasks rated as very to extremely important. Likewise, there is little variation in task frequency, with median values ranging from monthly to weekly.

Across all three IT work roles shown in Figures 3.15–3.17, we see that tasks were perceived as important to extremely important. Similar to the tasks for the Information Systems Secu-

---

[6] For a more complete list of KSATs for cybersecurity and cyberspace IT work roles, see DoD Cyber Exchange Public, 2020a; and DoD Cyber Exchange Public, 2020b.

FIGURE 3.14
Median Task Frequency and Importance, by KSAT, for Information Systems Security Manager (722) Across All Selected Organizations

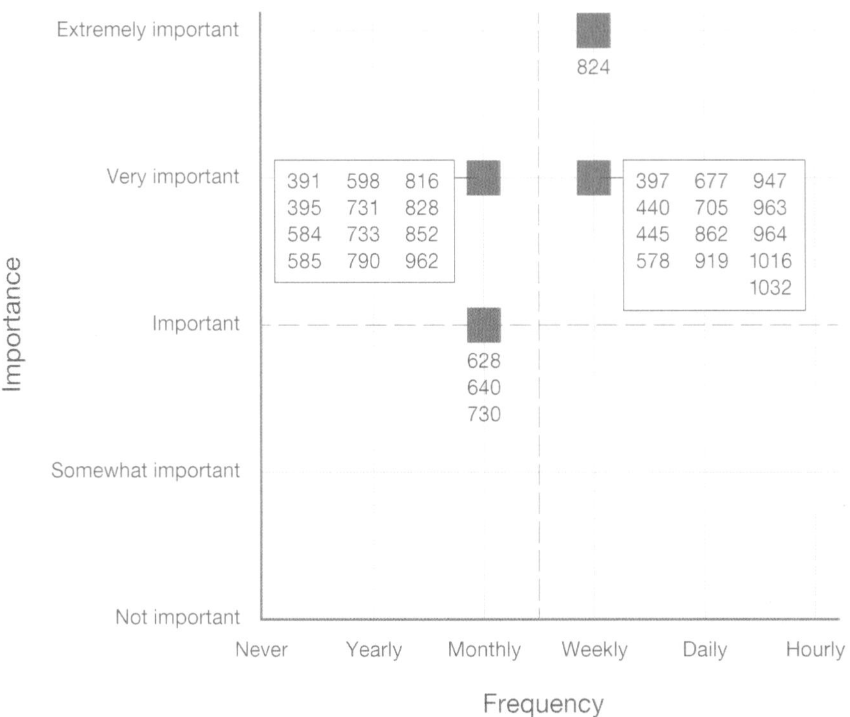

NOTE: Tasks are labeled according to KSAT code, per the DCWF taxonomy (DoD Cyber Exchange Public, 2020a). n = 172.

rity Manager (722) work role shown in Figure 3.14, most tasks for the three IT work roles were rated as very to extremely important. However, compared with the Information Systems Security Manager (722) tasks, we see more variation in task frequency among the three IT work roles, with median values ranging from yearly to daily. Again, we note that there is variation among the selected organizations, and although that level of detail is not shown in these figures, we did provide more detailed information directly to the services and DISA.

FIGURE 3.15
Median Task Frequency and Importance, by KSAT, for Technical Support Specialist (411) Across All Selected Organizations

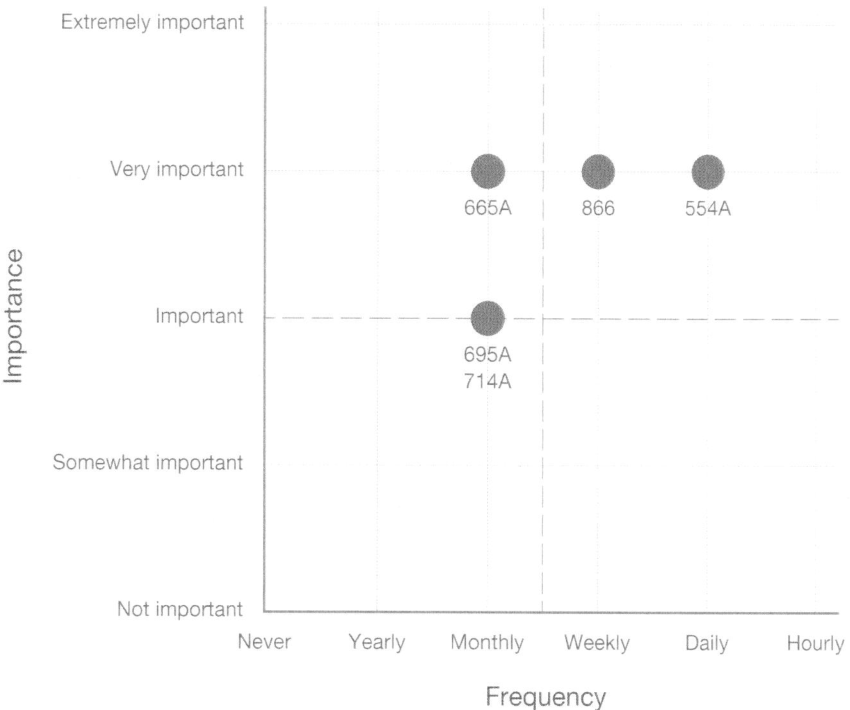

NOTE: Some tasks have identical values. Tasks are labeled according to KSAT code, per the DCWF taxonomy (DoD Cyber Exchange Public, 2020b). $n = 328$.

Manning and Capability Gaps

Insights on potential manning and capability gaps come from three sources. As described in Chapter Two, we conducted two analyses to compare the DoD and private sector cyber workforces. First, to compare *current staffing* of cyber personnel in the selected DoD organizations with the private sector, we used workforce data from the selected ZBR organizations and BLS. Second, to compare the *unfilled positions* for cyber personnel in the selected DoD organizations and the private sector, we used workforce data from the selected ZBR organizations and private sector job posting data from Burning Glass. The comparison using BLS data sheds light on the *distribution of personnel* across work roles, while the comparison using the Burning Glass data sheds light on the *distribution of manning gaps* across work roles.

FIGURE 3.16
Median Task Frequency and Importance, by KSAT, for Network Operations Specialist (441) Across All Selected Organizations

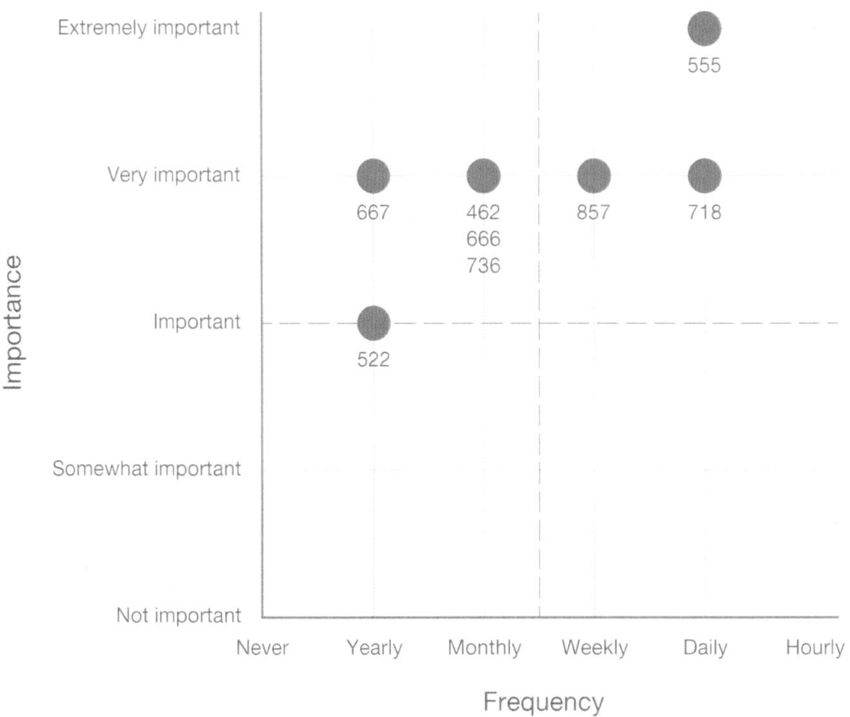

NOTE: Some tasks have identical values. Tasks are labeled according to KSAT code, per the DCWF taxonomy (DoD Cyber Exchange Public, 2020b). *n* = 152.

Lastly, we complement the DoD and private sector comparison with insights on manning and capability gaps gathered from the SME and deskside interviews.

Comparing Current Staffing in the Selected DoD Organizations and in the Private Sector

To compare current staffing, we needed a way to equate DCWF work roles and BLS standard occupational codes (SOCs).[7] We are not aware of an authoritative mapping between the two;

[7] The American Community Survey collects occupational data annually categorized by SOC defined in Office of Management and Budget, 2018.

FIGURE 3.17
Median Task Frequency and Importance, by KSAT, for System Administrator (451) Across All Selected Organizations

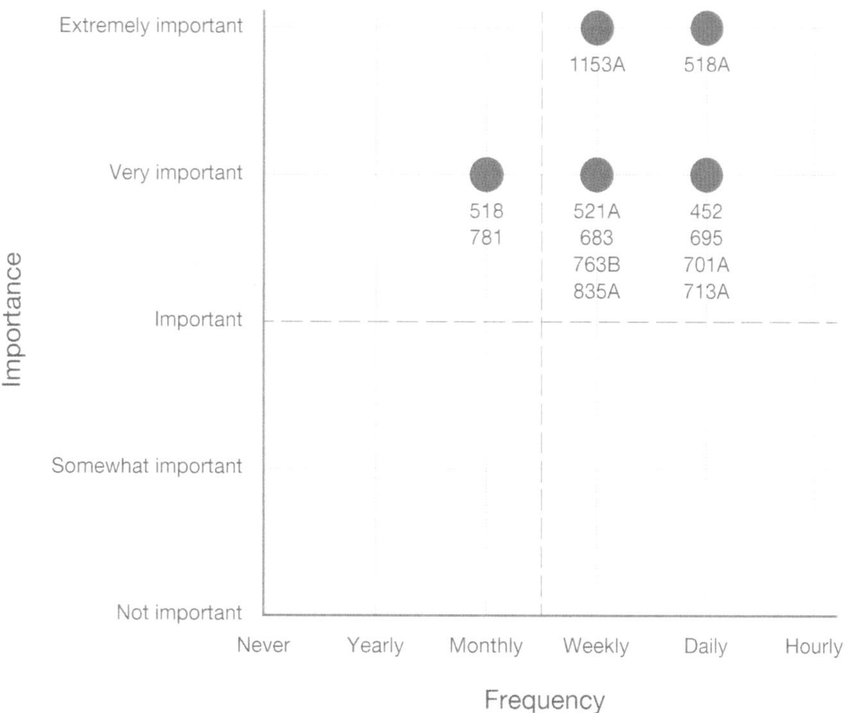

NOTE: Some tasks have identical values. Tasks are labeled according to KSAT code, per the DCWF taxonomy (DoD Cyber Exchange Public, 2020b). n = 256.

therefore, we created a crosswalk of DCWF work roles and BLS SOCs,[8] as shown in Table 3.1.[9] For the DCWF work roles, the work role number follows the work role title in parentheses. For BLS SOCs, the SOC code is listed first, followed by the SOC title.

With this mapping, we can compare current staffing by work role, as shown in Table 3.2. The first column shows the BLS SOC for all computer-related occupations tracked by BLS, while columns 2–5 show the percentage of personnel in that SOC as a share of all personnel in that sector, for each industry that most closely aligns with technology sectors—

[8] An alternative is the mapping method used by Markow and Vilvovsky, 2021, or Knapp et al., 2021, but these were outside the scope of this study. Although the Knapp et al. study used natural language–processing techniques, it still relied on SME input to resolve inconsistencies. It should be noted that repeatable computer techniques, such as latent semantic analysis (LSA), could be used to do a similar mapping. For more information on LSA, see Bennett and Landauer, 2000.

[9] We note that our mapping allows for a single SOC to be mapped to multiple DCWF work roles. We constrained the mapping such that multiple SOCs could not be mapped to a single DCWF work role. If an alternative method, such as natural language–processing is used, this constraint would be relaxed.

TABLE 3.1
Mapping BLS Standard Occupational Codes to DCWF Work Roles

DCWF Work Role	2018 BLS SOC
Cybersecurity	
• Cyber Defense Forensics Analyst (212)	• 15-1212 Information Security Analyst
• Systems Security Analyst (461)	• 15-1212 Information Security Analyst
• Cyber Defense Analyst (511)	• 15-1212 Information Security Analyst
• Cyber Defense Infrastructure Support Specialist (521)	• 15-1212 Information Security Analyst
• Cyber Defense Incident Responder (531)	• 15-1212 Information Security Analyst
• Vulnerability Assessment Analyst (541)	• 15-1212 Information Security Analyst
• Security Control Assessor (612)	• 15-1212 Information Security Analyst
• Information Systems Security Developer (631)	• 11-3021 Computer and Information Systems Manager
• Security Architect (652)	• 11-3021 Computer and Information Systems Manager
• Authorizing Official/Designating Representative (611)	• 11-3021 Computer and Information Systems Manager
• Secure Software Assessor (622)	• 15-1256 Software Developers and Software Quality Assurance Analyst and Tester
• Information Systems Security Manager (722)	• 11-3021 Computer and Information Systems Manager
• COMSEC Manager (723)	• 11-3021 Computer and Information Systems Manager
IT	
• Technical Support Specialist (411)	• 15-1232 Computer User Support Specialist
• Database Administrator (421)	• 15-1232 Computer User Support Specialist
• Data Analyst (422)	• 15-2098 Data Scientists and Mathematical Science Occupations, All Other
• Knowledge Manager (431)	• 11-3021 Computer and Information Systems Manager
• Network Operations Specialist (441)	• 15-1231 Computer Network Support Specialist
• System Administrator (451)	• 15-1244 Network and Computer Systems Administrator
• Software Developer (621)	• 15-1251 Computer Programmer
• Systems Developer (632)	• 17-2061 Computer Hardware Engineer
• Systems Requirements Planner (641)	• 17-2061 Computer Hardware Engineer
• Enterprise Architect (651)	• 15-1241 Computer Network Architect

Table 3.1—Continued

DCWF Work Role	2018 BLS SOC
• Research and Development Specialist (661)	• 15-1221 Computer and Information Research Scientist
• System Testing and Evaluation Specialist (671)	• 15-1211 Computer Systems Analyst

SOURCE: Authors' analysis of DoD Cyber Exchange Public, 2020a; DoD Cyber Exchange Public, 2020b; and Office of Management and Budget, 2018.

NOTE: We did not include the following seven computer- or security-related SOCs in our mapping because they were not well aligned to DCWF skills and functions: 15-1257 Web Developers and Digital Interface Designers, 49-2022 Telecommunications Equipment Installers and Repairers, except Line Installers, 15-2011 Actuaries, 15-2021 Mathematicians, 15-2031 Operations Research Analysts, 15-2041 Statisticians, and 15-1299 Computer Occupations, All Other.

TABLE 3.2

Comparison of BLS Data with Mapped DCWF Work Roles

	Percentage of Personnel in SOC Among Personnel in					
SOC	Information Sector (%)	Finance and Insurance Sector (%)	PSS Sector (%)	All Sectors (%)	Mapped DCWF Work Role(s)	Percentage of DoD Personnel in ZBR Orgs (%)
11-3021	9	13	9	10	431, 611, 631, 652, 722, 723	13
15-1211	7	19	13	11	671	5
15-1212	2	7	5	5	212, 461, 511, 521, 531, 541, 612	10
15-1221	4	N/A	2	3	661	2
15-1231	7	4	3	6	441	11
15-1232	13	8	12	10	411	26
15-1241	5	4	4	6	651	2
15-1244	6	7	6	6	451	12
15-1245	3	4	2	3	421	2
15-1251	4	3	5	6	621	8
15-1256	37	32	33	28	622	0[a]
15-2098	1	0	2	2	422	1
17-2061	3	0	3	4	632, 641	11

SOURCE: Authors' analysis of May 2020 Occupational Employment and Wage Statistics data (BLS, undated).

NOTE: BLS data are computer-related SOCs as a percentage of the total computer-related SOCs for companies having equal to or greater than 1,000 employees. See Table 3.1 for the titles associated with each SOC and DCWF work role number. N/A = no data; PSS = professional, scientific, and technical services; ZBR Orgs = participating DoD organizations.

[a] Only 57 of 16,928 DoD personnel held this work role.

information, finance and insurance, and PSS—as well as an aggregate view of all sectors.[10] Column 6 shows the mapped DCWF work roles (in some cases, a given SOC may map to multiple DCWF roles), and the last column shows the percentage of DoD personnel performing the given role(s) among all cybersecurity and IT personnel from the selected ZBR organizations.[11] For example, 7 percent of personnel in computer-related SOCs in the information sector are 15-1211 Computer Systems Analysts, whereas 5 percent of all cybersecurity and IT personnel from the DoD organizations selected to participate in the ZBR perform the related System Testing and Evaluation Specialist (671) DCWF work role.

Based on these data, private industry values range from near 0 percent (15-2098 Data Scientist and 17-2061 Computer Hardware Engineer in the finance and insurance sector) to 37 percent (15-1256 Software Developers and Software Quality Assurance Analysts and Testers in the information sector). On the other hand, allocations for personnel in selected DoD organizations range from zero (Secure Software Assessor [622]) to 26 percent (Technical Support Specialist [411]).

When comparing the results for personnel from sectors shown in columns 2–5 with those for personnel in the ZBR organizations (column 7), several differences are apparent. Endpoint-facing work roles, such as Network Operations Specialist (441) and Technical Support Specialist (411), comprise a larger share of the cyber workforce in the selected DoD organizations than in their corresponding BLS SOCs: 15-1231 Computer Network Support Specialists and 15-1232 Computer User Support Specialists. Conversely, the share of the DoD cyber workforce in the DCWF Secure Software Assessor (622) work role is lower than it is for its corresponding BLS SOC, 15-1256 Software Developers and Software Quality Assurance Analysts and Testers. This is possibly due to the broad set of job titles within the 15-1256 SOC.

Comparing Unfilled Positions in the Selected DoD Organizations and in the Private Sector

To compare unfilled positions for cyber personnel in the selected DoD organizations and the private sector, we reviewed private and public sector job posting data from Burning Glass with information on workforce gaps collected during the ZBR. The job posting data capture the distribution of job postings, by work role, that reflect what the private and public sectors are looking to hire, while the workforce data from the selected DoD organizations allow us to identify the distribution of gapped positions, by work role, that selected organizations are looking to fill. The graphical results are shown in Figure 3.18. The data are also provided in Table D.2 in Appendix D.

---

[10] The North American Industry Classification System (NAICS) assigns the following numbers to these industry sectors: information (NAICS 51), finance and insurance (NAICS 52), and professional, scientific, and technical services (NAICS 54).

[11] Note that this comparison is approximate because the mapping of BLS SOC to DCWF work role is not unique and that the DoD data represent just a subset of all DoD cyber personnel.

FIGURE 3.18

Comparing the Distribution of Private and Public Sector Job Postings with the Distribution of Unfilled Positions in DoD Organizations Selected to Participate in the ZBR, by Cybersecurity and IT Work Role

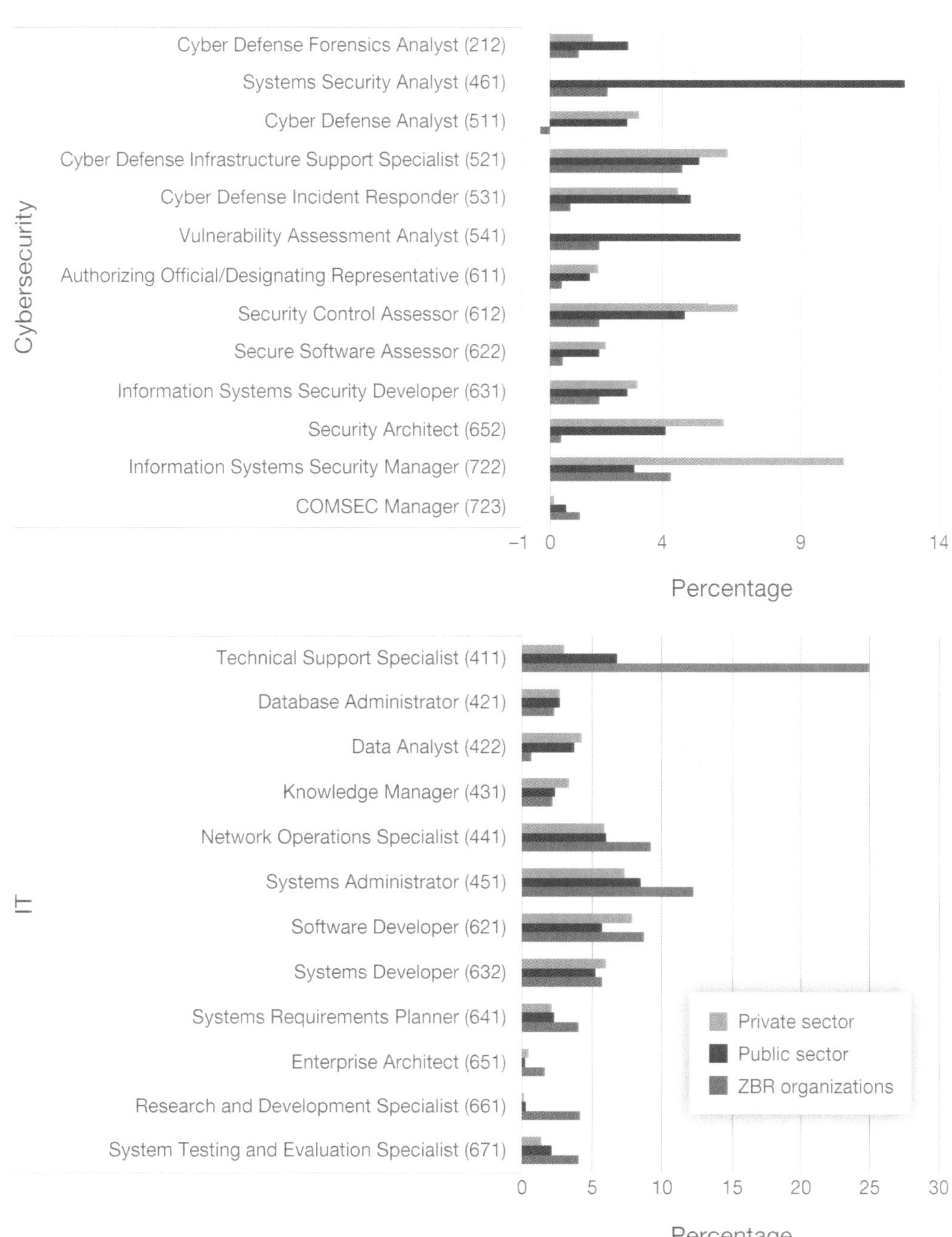

SOURCE: Authors' analysis of April 2020 to March 2021 NIST data (CyberSeek, undated), as well as distribution list data collected from the selected DoD organizations. See Table D.2 for a tabular version of these data.

NOTE: Percentages are shown as a share of all job postings or all unfilled positions, as the case may be, across all work roles.

Overall, the distributions of private and public sector job postings tend to be more similar to each other than they are to the distribution of unfilled positions in the DoD organizations selected to participate in the ZBR. Moreover, six cybersecurity work roles and one IT work role comprise a much smaller share of unfilled positions at ZBR organizations compared with their share of private and public sector job postings: Data Analyst (422), Systems Security Analyst (461), Cyber Defense Analyst (511), Cyber Defense Incident Responder (531), Vulnerability Assessment Analyst (541), Security Control Assessor (612), and Security Architect (652). On the other hand, four IT work roles comprise a much larger share of unfilled positions at ZBR organizations compared with their share of private and public sector job postings: Technical Support Specialist (411), Network Operations Specialist (441), System Administrator (451), and Research and Development Specialist (661).

These data suggest that the DoD organizations selected to participate in the ZBR are generally more undermanned among IT work roles (in particular, the Technical Support Specialist [411]), relative to private and public sector organizations. This could be explained by a difference in the missions of the organizations; for instance, the mission of the selected ZBR organizations could be more focused on IT operations and maintenance than on cybersecurity tasks, such as security architecture or incident response. In addition, DoD missions may require personnel to be forward deployed or situated in less desirable locations, increasing the difficulty of filling entry level roles, such as the Technical Support Specialist (411). Alternatively, the selected DoD organizations may be better able to fill cybersecurity work roles, relative to IT work roles. In addition, demand for the Technical Support Specialist (411) skill set in the private and public sector is possibly being met (thereby driving down the number of job postings), or differences in the efficiency of Technical Support Specialists across the private, public, and DoD organizations may explain these results.

Insights on Manning and Capability Gaps from the Subject-Matter Expert and Deskside Interviews

In addition to the comparisons of the DoD and private sector cyber workforces, we also collected information in the SME and deskside interviews that pertains to manning and capability gaps. A common manning topic among personnel at all selected organizations was the belief that both the cybersecurity and IT functional areas were undermanned. Several participants also reported that recruitment and retention challenges contribute to manning and capability gaps, despite the initiatives designed to make military services more competitive with employers from the private sector or from other parts of the U.S. government. A smaller number of participants also suggested that the mix of people and skills may not be aligned with their assigned cyber missions; for example, personnel assigned a single work role undertake tasks assigned to other work roles, or personnel lack the proper training, especially on the tools that they are expected to use.

A common capability topic among participants were issues with software tool management. For example, some tools are acquired and used for a single purpose, whereas making the tool widely available could significantly increase an organization's efficiency and effectiveness. Moreover, participants noted that slow acquisition and deployment cycles, as well as inaccessible and inadequate user training, limited a new tool's impact. Some participants expressed a concern that failure to identify future technology trends and needs can cause organizations to operate less efficiently and effectively compared with leading industry firms, regardless of whether the workforce primarily consists of civilians or contractors. A less common topic of concern was the heavy reliance on contractors.[12] For example, participants noted an inability to enforce minimum and consistent skill requirements in the contract, the inability to prescribe the execution of activities, gaps in support during contract renewal, and the loss of corporate knowledge if contracted expertise is not retained.

Potential Barriers to Efficiency and Effectiveness

Information about potential barriers to workplace efficiency and effectiveness come from three sources: the data call and the SME and deskside interviews. As noted in the protocols for the data call and interviews (see Appendixes A–C), for the purpose of this discussion, we define *efficient* as leading to the least amount of waste and *effective* as successfully producing the desired result.

In the data call, respondents were asked about barriers to efficiency and effectiveness pertaining to their work roles, and we coded their responses based on the following nine topics that emerged from the data call: tools and technology, budget, process, policy, communication, leadership, training, personnel, and the workplace. Overall, participants mentioned these topics with about the same frequency across ZBR organizations. That is, the share of responses for all selected organizations involved topics relating to process (from 20 percent to 30 percent of responses) and tools and technology (from 15 percent to 25 percent of responses). Topics relating to policy, training, and personnel were mentioned roughly 5 percent to 15 percent of the time, while topics relating to budget, communication, leadership, and the workplace were mentioned the least often, about 5 percent of the time, on average, for all ZBR organizations.

We used the information gathered in the data call and in the SME and deskside interviews to flesh out these topics, turning our attention first to the most common topic from the data call: process. Personnel described processes as "burdensome" and "slow," and they mentioned that excessive bureaucracy and administration restricted the staff's ability to perform their work. Personnel stated that there is too much repetition in their work and identified spe-

[12] Contractors were not included in the ZBR data collection (i.e., SME interviews, work analysis data call, and deskside interviews). Nonetheless, contractors were frequently mentioned during our data collection by military and civilian participants.

cific processes that needed to be streamlined, such as the Risk Management Framework, the System Authorization Access Request, and processing that occurs during testing and evaluation. They further stated that they suffer from a lack of information and that a centralized database would improve processes. Personnel also stated that work roles and the delineation of work tasks are often not clear and job tasks need to clearly identify who is responsible for performing the task.

For the second most common topic from the data call, tools and technology, personnel reported a lack of up-to-date tools and technology (e.g., developer tools, computer hardware, and software) necessary to complete their jobs. Personnel also cited issues with network connectivity, virtual private networks, and remote desktop connections, and they mentioned a need for the automation of work role tasks and better access to cloud services to improve efficiency and effectiveness.

Other commonly mentioned topics were policy and training. Regarding policy, personnel cited difficulty managing an overabundance of polices, specifically those governing acquisition and system testing. One participant stated, "The policy structure is too complex and prevents work from getting done as programs attempt to navigate the maze." Policy discrepancies and misalignment between service and DoD policy were also raised as barriers to efficiency and effectiveness.

Comments on training focused on the suitability of training to the cyber tasks for which personnel were routinely responsible. Personnel suggested that centralizing training would help ensure that they received the necessary training for their roles. Personnel also suggested that training was the most significant barrier to ensuring that the cybersecurity and IT workforces were effective and efficient. Initial skills training is needed, especially for military personnel, to provide foundational skills. Moreover, recurring and continued training was discussed as being necessary to maintain proficiency and keep pace with industry. Personnel stated that new staff were often poorly trained, undertrained, or did not possess the necessary certifications to perform their jobs. High turnover rates additionally contributed to poorly trained personnel. Personnel also commented that access to private sector training would help newer personnel. Lastly, personnel reported that they needed training for software tools that are not part of initial or continuation training, as well as training for any new tools and technologies being acquired.[13]

[13] Although the influx of early career civilians may enable DoD to inherit some experience with industry or academic standard tools, many tasks are performed with mature and tailored tools unique to DoD. Those same early career civilians may have limited opportunities for training that takes them away from their daily tasking. On-the-job training mitigates this but may not be sufficient because of limited corporate knowledge of tools and techniques. Formal training is needed where over-the-shoulder training cannot adequately provide the requisite skill sets needed. Finally, respondents noted that knowledge management (e.g., lessons learned, helpdesk records, and standard operating procedures) could be greatly improved, noting that it was often siloed or ad hoc.

Comments about budget, communication, leadership, and the workplace were less common. Inadequate budgets were cited as the reason for personnel having to use older software tools, with one respondent stating that the

> lack of funding leads to lapses in support as well as aging equipment that requires more and more time to maintain instead of operate and [that] leads to unpatched programs that open up vulnerabilities in network operations or downtime due to required updates that are not able to be performed.

Comments about leadership and communication were related; personnel expressed a desire that leadership take a more active role and provide more guidance and more direction on mission priorities and maintaining cybersecurity standards. Workplace issues were predominately related to a desire to maintain telework options to enhance productivity and work-life balance.

Potential Future Changes in Work Performed or Requirements

In the SME and deskside interviews, participants were asked whether they anticipate future changes in the work that they perform or manpower requirements. Questions addressed factors that will significantly change the workload, organizational changes, new tools and technologies, changes to manpower mixes and budgets, and the potential for technology or automation to affect future workforce needs. Insights gathered from the SME and deskside interview participants coalesced around a small number of consistent topics.

A near universal topic was that improved and emerging technologies, such as industrial control systems, remote endpoint management, and cloud services, will result in future work changes, which will require additional training and expertise. A related finding is that the relationship between DoD organizations and IT vendors may demand greater technical oversight to ensure vendor accountability. For example, the complexity of cloud security may well require a sophisticated workforce to properly manage it, even if the cloud platform is provided and operated by an external vendor.

Another common topic was that the introduction of IT automation is expected to increase the frequency and quantity of data collected, which will result in a larger data analysis workload that requires different skills, such as data science and data governance. The final topic that participants mentioned concerned the growing threat from nation-states, which must be considered in predicting which additional tasking, skills, and tools would be needed to adequately secure, detect, and defend the growing number of DoD networks and endpoints.

CHAPTER FOUR

Discussion

In this report, we have presented findings based on multiple data sources and research methods to help inform the ZBR of DoD cybersecurity and IT personnel as required by the FY 2020 NDAA. We aggregated the findings across ten organizations selected to participate in the ZBR and organized them by five main themes that capture the NDAA's key task requirements. In addition to the findings, this report also documents a transparent and repeatable process for continuing ZBR initiatives across the DoD cyber enterprise. In this concluding chapter, we interlace a discussion of the repeatable process with the findings that it produced for the selected organizations, organized around each of the five main themes.

For the first theme, *current workforce*, we analyzed personnel and requirements information from the selected organizations for all DCWF cybersecurity and IT work roles. These data enabled us to examine and visualize the size of the workforce and workforce gaps, by work role, across the organizations. Even this simple, aggregated information will prove useful for the selected organizations, which are not in a position to routinely gather these data. We used the personnel and requirements data to identify those work roles with large and small numbers of personnel and those that suffer from large or small workforce gaps. We supplemented the personnel and requirements data with an analysis of a sample of civilian PDs provided by the selected organizations. The PD analysis allowed us to better understand the degree to which personnel management at the selected organizations is aligned with the DCWF. The alignment of PDs with the DCWF will become more critical as DoD continues to adopt and implement work role coding to aid in the management of its cyber workforce.

The next theme, *current work performed*, sought to understand the activities and tempo of work performed by DoD cyber personnel. Specifically, we captured information about the frequency and importance of the tasks completed by personnel in cybersecurity and IT work roles in the selected organizations. This analysis helped identify tasks that are performed more or less frequently, as well as respondents' views of how important these tasks are to the success of their missions. This information may prove useful to workforce managers as they assess how some work roles may be susceptible to burnout or attrition (because of high tempo) or which work roles and associated tasks may require more training (because of infrequent execution). We acknowledge that this analysis, however, does not capture task duration, which could explain some of the differences in how frequently tasks are performed.

The third theme, *manning and capability gaps*, was assessed through insights collected from a comparison between DoD and private sector cyber workforces and through SME interviews. We compared information about current staffing and unfilled positions across cybersecurity and IT work roles with the private sector by using BLS data and publicly available job postings data, respectively. Although there are many challenges with comparing workforce data between private and public sectors, the analysis that we conducted provides an approximate understanding of the differences and similarities in how these workforces resource cybersecurity and IT tasks, functions, and roles. Cyber workforce managers should find the current staffing data helpful as a snapshot of current manning and capability gaps and the job postings data to help inform current and projected workforce hiring.

The fourth and fifth themes, *potential barriers to efficiency and effectiveness* and *potential future changes in work performed or requirements*, were both informed through SME interviews at the selected organizations. We coded SME insights into common topic areas to provide the interested researcher, workforce manager, or DoD leadership with a narrative about the most common or pressing issues facing the cybersecurity and IT workforces at the selected organizations.

We close with a discussion of the role that key stakeholders played in the ZBR process. In addition to the research described in this report, the entire ZBR effort required participation from dozens of stakeholders across DoD, who each performed a vital role. To give the reader a sense of the magnitude of this collective effort, we will describe some of the instrumental actions taken by key stakeholders; however, this is not an exhaustive list.

The Tri-Chair, composed of representatives from PCA, DoD CIO, and USD P&R, provided the strategic vision for the ZBR and guided its execution throughout. The Tri-Chair assembled representatives from each of the services and DISA, established a working group meeting tempo, and ensured interim deliverables were produced and coordinated with all relevant parties. The Tri-Chair also created and fielded a workforce census that was key to the current workforce analysis described in this report, and it interfaced with DoD union representatives to ensure appropriate delivery of the data call. The Tri-Chair is also ultimately responsible for reviewing and certifying the ZBR submissions provided by the services and DISA, providing recommendations based on their findings, overseeing the implementation of those recommendations, and communicating the results of the ZBR effort to Congress.

The services and DISA were consistently represented in working group discussions throughout the duration of the ZBR, assuming responsibility for communicating timelines and deliverables throughout their organizations and to their leadership. The services and DISA were given the freedom to choose how to proceed within each of their organizations, which involved identifying the complete email distribution lists of cybersecurity and IT personnel within their organizations; fielding the data call to all cybersecurity and IT personnel and working to ensure maximum participation; identifying appropriate personnel for us to interview; providing us with supporting documentation (e.g., civilian PDs) for analysis; conducting briefings to update their leadership; and finally, writing, coordinating, and delivering their own ZBRs to the Tri-Chair.

The process of identifying cybersecurity and IT personnel and, more generally, educating personnel on the DCWF proved challenging for most organizations. Although the DCWF has been formally adopted by DoD, it is still largely underused across DoD. In some cases, cybersecurity and IT personnel participating in the ZBR data collection had difficulty recognizing and linking the specific tasks that they perform with a formal DCWF work role. That being said, it appears that the execution of the ZBR acted as a forcing function to help increase awareness of the DCWF across the participating organizations.

Together with the actions taken by the Tri-Chair, the services, and DISA, the research documented in this report constitutes a transparent, objective, and repeatable process through which DoD can continue to conduct ZBRs across the cyber enterprise.

APPENDIX A

Subject-Matter Expert Interview Protocol

This appendix reproduces the protocol that we designed to conduct SME interviews with each of the organizations selected to participate in the ZBR.

Study Background and Purpose

The FY 2020 National Defense Authorization Act calls for a review of U.S. Department of Defense (DoD) cybersecurity and cyberspace IT personnel to be submitted to and jointly reviewed by the Principal Cyber Advisor, the DoD Chief Information Officer, and the Under Secretary of Defense for Personnel and Readiness. RAND's National Defense Research Institute (NDRI) has been asked to conduct research in support of this review. Specifically, RAND NDRI has been asked to validate and ensure the consistency of the data and analysis used by the departments, components, or agencies for organizations submitting reviews.

As part of the RAND NDRI effort, we are conducting interviews with leadership and supervisors of cybersecurity and cyberspace IT personnel in your organization to better understand

- the cybersecurity and cyberspace IT workforce and workload
- cybersecurity and cyberspace IT workforce staffing numbers
- potential barriers to effectiveness and efficiency of the cybersecurity and cyberspace IT work being performed
- potential future changes in cybersecurity and cyberspace IT workload or requirements.

Throughout this discussion, we will refer to the DoD Cyber Workforce Framework (DCWF), which is a taxonomy of work roles that includes specialty areas and tasks for DoD cyber jobs.[1] For definitions of the cybersecurity and cyberspace IT workforces, we reference DoD Directive (DoDD) 8140.01, *Cyberspace Workforce Management*:[2]

---

[1] For more information on the DCWF, see DoD Cyber Exchange Public, undated-b. For more information on cybersecurity and cyberspace IT work roles, see DoD Cyber Exchange Public, 2020a; and DoD Cyber Exchange Public, 2020b.

[2] DoDD 8140.01, *Cyberspace Workforce Management*, Washington, D.C.: Office of the DoD Chief Information Officer, October 5, 2020, pp. 11–12.

> Cybersecurity workforce: Personnel who secure, defend, and preserve data, networks, net-centric capabilities, and other designated systems by ensuring appropriate security controls and measures are in place, and taking internal defense actions. This includes access to system controls, monitoring, administration, and integration of cybersecurity into all aspects of engineering and acquisition of cyberspace capabilities.
>
> Cyberspace IT workforce: Personnel who design, build, configure, operate, and maintain IT, networks, and capabilities. This includes actions to prioritize portfolio investments; architect, engineer, acquire, implement, evaluate, and dispose of IT as well as information resource management; and the management, storage, transmission, and display of data and information.

Also, when we mention contractors, we are referring to contractors who are a full-time equivalent workers associated or embedded with the organization who fill a specific cybersecurity or cyberspace IT support billet or are required to complete essential cybersecurity or cyberspace IT tasks. We are *not* referring to contractors who are providing a contracted service (i.e., temporary workers who are not associated with the organization and who provide a short-term or specific instance of a service).

Participation

Your participation in this discussion is entirely voluntary. You can choose not to participate or skip any points that you would rather not discuss. Additionally, if at any time you no longer want to participate, just let us know, and we can stop the conversation.

How We Will Use the Information That You Provide

During our discussion, we will be taking notes so we can accurately capture your comments for our analyses. In any briefings and reports that we produce, we will combine the information that you provide with information that we receive from other representatives from your organization. We may include some direct quotes in our briefings and reports, but we will not attribute them to anyone by name or in a way that would directly identify you. Please let us know if there is anything that you want us to keep off the record and not quote.

Your name and position will be recorded with the notes that we take and keep in our research files to show that we talked to individuals with critical knowledge and to assist with any follow-up that may be needed. For any briefings and reports that we produce, your name will not be included; however, your position will be included in a list of participants. Are you comfortable having your position included in a list of participants in our briefings and reports?

Discussion Questions

General Background Questions

1. Could you start by giving us a brief description of your position and responsibilities?
   a. What is your background and experience prior to your current position?
   b. How long have you been in your current position?

Organizational Background and Structure

2. Can you briefly describe your organization's mission?
3. How are your organization's cybersecurity and cyberspace IT functions organized?
4. Can you briefly describe how the structure of your organization's cybersecurity and cyberspace IT functions came to be?
   a. Has anything significantly changed in how your organization has structured and organized the cybersecurity and cyberspace IT functions?

Cybersecurity and Cyberspace IT Workforce and Workload

5. How does your organization determine the number and type of billets that it needs to accomplish the cybersecurity and cyberspace IT mission?
   a. How do you prioritize filling those billets?
   b. How do you divide the workload between military and civilian personnel and contractors?
   c. Are there specific roles that contractors fill compared with military and civilian personnel and why?
6. How do the current functions and personnel in your organization fit into DoD's cyber security architecture (i.e., enterprise-wide efforts and missions)? How do they support the Cyber Mission Force mission/construct? What other DoD organizations do you interact with in performing your cybersecurity or cyberspace IT duties and for what tasks/roles?
7. When you think about the kind of cybersecurity and cyberspace IT work that is done in your organization, how is it different than the work performed at your higher headquarters (e.g., service headquarters, combatant command headquarters)? Differences can include type of work, scope, amount, etc.
   a. What, if any, overlaps exist in the work performed?
8. In your experience, are the civilian position descriptions (PDs) or military occupational specialties/subspecialties associated with cybersecurity and cyberspace IT billets a good indication of the work being performed?
   a. If not, why? Can you provide some examples of a mismatch between the civilian PD/military occupational specialties/subspecialties associated with the billet and the work being performed?

   b. How up to date and relevant are the civilian PDs/military occupational specialties/subspecialties associated with the billets?

9. Are you familiar with the DoD Cyber Workforce Framework (DCWF)? [*Interviewer: If not, refer back to the short description of the DCWF in the introduction section before asking the following.*] To what extent has your organization adopted the DCWF?
   a. Does the DCWF fully capture the cybersecurity and cyberspace IT work being performed at your organization? If not, what does the DCWF not capture?
   b. Have the cybersecurity and cyberspace IT billets been coded according to the DCWF?
   c. Do civilian PDs/military occupational specialties/subspecialties align with work roles described in the DCWF?

Cybersecurity and Cyberspace IT Workforce Staffing Numbers

10. Do you consider your organization to be undermanned in terms of cybersecurity or cyberspace IT personnel? *If yes/affirmative response:*
    a. Are there any commonalities among the unfilled billets? For instance, are they mostly military, civilian, or contractor? Are they mostly junior or senior pay grades?
    b. Can you provide specific examples of billets that are not filled? Are some billets persistently hard to fill?
    c. What has led to the undermanning (e.g., recruiting/retention challenges, mismatch in skill or experience levels, security clearance process)?
    d. Could technology or automation help mitigate any of these workforce gaps? If so, how? (*Example: new software that can automate certain cybersecurity/cyberspace IT activities*)
11. Do you have any cybersecurity or cyberspace IT personnel who are working in your organization but are on loan from other organizations? If so, about how many and for what work roles/position types? What about the opposite, people who are assigned to your organization but are on loan to other organizations?
12. What, if any, types of competencies or capabilities are you currently missing from your organization's cybersecurity and cyberspace IT workforce? *If missing competencies/capabilities are provided:*
    a. What factors affect what is missing from this workforce? (*Examples: limited supply of certain types of talent in civilian and military labor pools, i.e., recruiting/retention [to include concerns over pay]; slow hiring process for civilians; training delays*)
13. Are there any areas in which your organization is overmanned in terms of cybersecurity and cyberspace IT personnel? *If yes/affirmative response:*

a. Are there any commonalities among the excess personnel? For instance, are they mostly military, civilian, or contractor? Are they mostly junior or senior pay grades?
b. What has led to the overmanning (e.g., technology changes, mismatch in skill or experience levels)?

Potential Barriers to Effectiveness and Efficiency of the Cybersecurity and Cyberspace IT Work Being Performed

14. In addition to gaps in the number and type of people, are there other barriers to how effectively[3] and efficiently personnel in these cybersecurity or cyberspace IT positions in your organization perform their work? *If yes/affirmative response:*
    a. What are those barriers (e.g., lacking resources, to include specific technology; operational restrictions; limitations on authorities; insufficient training; issues with the assignment or allocation of tasks; insufficient standard operating procedures, job aids, or manuals; challenges that arise due to working on classified information or in a classified facility)?
    b. Are there activities that are particularly time intensive or complex that could be made more efficient or effective by the introduction of new technology?
15. How does your organization think about or determine whether cybersecurity or cyberspace IT work is being done efficiently? How work is being done effectively?
    a. Do you have ways to capture effectiveness? Or efficiency?

Potential Future Changes in Cybersecurity and Cyberspace IT Workload or Requirements

16. Do you anticipate any significant changes to your organization's workload in the next few years? *If yes/affirmative response:*
    a. What factors will significantly change the workload? *Probes (examples if they have trouble responding):*
        i. Change in organizational authorities, structures, and/or missions?
        ii. Acquisition or development of tools, applications, or other technological capabilities?
        iii. Manpower budget/funding level changes?
17. What do you anticipate your organization will need in terms of the number and mix of civilian/military/contractor personnel for cybersecurity or cyberspace IT functions in the next five years?

[3] For the purposes of this discussion, we define *effective* as successfully producing the desired result and *efficient* as leading to the least amount of waste.

a. What do you anticipate needing in terms of the mix of skills (i.e., competencies or capabilities)?
b. How might technology or automation affect your future workforce needs?

Closing Questions

18. Is there anything we have not discussed related to the cybersecurity or cyberspace IT workforces that you think we should be aware of as we move forward with our study?
19. Are there other individuals or stakeholders you would suggest we speak with for our study?
20. Are there relevant reports or materials that you could share with us?

APPENDIX B

Work Analysis Data Call Protocol

This appendix reproduces the protocol that we designed for the data call that the Tri-Chair administered through MAX.gov to each of the organizations selected to participate in the ZBR.

DoD Cybersecurity and Cyberspace Information Technology Workforce Data Call

We are asking for your help in better understanding the work performed by the cybersecurity and cyberspace information technology (IT) workforce in the U.S. Department of Defense (DoD). Section 1652 of the FY 2020 National Defense Authorization Act (NDAA) directs DoD to perform a zero-based review (ZBR) of its cybersecurity and cyberspace IT workforce. This data call is meant to support the ZBR effort.

How was I chosen? You are being asked to complete this data call because you are in a cybersecurity or cyberspace IT position in an organization that is participating in the ZBR effort. Participation is voluntary, but we hope you will help in this important effort.

What does participation involve? The data call contains questions about cybersecurity and cyberspace IT work roles and the types of tasks performed in those work roles. The data call should take roughly 15 minutes to complete.

What will be done with my survey responses? All individual responses will be anonymous; please do not provide identifying information, such as your name, as part of your answers on the data call. Your responses will be combined with information from other respondents for final analyses. Comments written in response to open-ended questions (free-form text fields) may be reported word for word but never with identifiable information.

About Your Job

Q01

Please select the agency/branch of service that is your employer.

1. 4th Estate (DISA)
2. Air Force
3. Army

4. Navy
5. Marine Corps
6. Other (*free-form text field*)

Q02
Please select the organization where you physically work in a cybersecurity or cyberspace IT position.

1. DISA (including JFHQ DoDIN)
2. Air Force, Air Force Materiel Command (AF1M)
3. Army, U.S. Army Cyber Command (AR2A)
4. Army, U.S. Army Communications Electronics Command (ARX8)
5. Navy, Naval Information Warfare Systems Command (NAVWARSYSCOM, NAVWAR, NV39)
6. Navy, NETWARCOM
7. USMC, MCIWEST MCB CAMPEN G-6
8. USMC, Marine Corps Cyberspace Ops Group (MCCOG)
9. USMC, 1st Network Bn
10. Other (*free-form text field*)

Q03
For this organization, are you serving as an officer, warrant officer, enlisted, civilian, or contractor?

1. Commissioned officer
2. Warrant officer
3. Enlisted
4. Civilian
5. Contractor (*if chosen, send respondent to exit page*)

Q04
Please select your pay grade.

If "commissioned officer" is selected	If "warrant officer" is selected	If "enlisted" is selected	If "civilian" is selected
O1	WO1	E1	GS/GG 5 or equivalent
O2	CW2/CWO2	E2	GS/GG 6 or equivalent
O3	CW3/CWO3	E3	GS/GG 7 or equivalent
O4	CW4/CWO4	E4	GS/GG 8 or equivalent
O5	CW5/CWO5	E5	GS/GG 9 or equivalent
O6		E6	GS/GG 10 or equivalent
O7		E7	GS/GG 11 or equivalent

If "commissioned officer" is selected	If "warrant officer" is selected	If "enlisted" is selected	If "civilian" is selected
O8		E8	GS/GG 12 or equivalent
O9		E9	GS/GG 13 or equivalent
			GS/GG 14 or equivalent
			GS/GG 15 or equivalent
			SES or equivalent (e.g., ST)
			Other

Q05
Please select your occupational specialty (*free-form text field*).

Q06
How long have you been in your current position?

1. Less than 6 months
2. 6–12 months
3. 12+ months

Q07
How long have you been working in cybersecurity or cyberspace IT, including your current position? Please include work experience in both the private and the government sectors.

1. Less than 6 months
2. 6–12 months
3. 1–5 years
4. 6–10 years
5. More than 10 years

Q08
The DoD Cyber Workforce Framework (DCWF) includes specialty areas, workforce elements, work roles, and tasks for DoD cyber jobs. Below are DCWF work roles. Please select your *primary* and *secondary* (if applicable) work role. When you think about your *primary* and *secondary* (if applicable) work role, think about the work that you do in a typical workweek.

If none of the work roles apply to your current position, please select "None of these work roles apply." [*Skip to Q10*]

Cybersecurity Work Roles	Primary	Secondary
Cyber Defense Forensics Analyst (212)		
Systems Security Analyst (461)		

Cybersecurity Work Roles	Primary	Secondary
Cyber Defense Analyst (511)		
Cyber Defense Infrastructure Support Specialist (521)		
Cyber Defense Incident Responder (531)		
Vulnerability Assessment Analyst (541)		
Authorizing Official/Designating Representative (611)		
Security Control Assessor (612)		
Secure Software Assessor (622)		
Information Systems Security Developer (631)		
Security Architect (652)		
Information Systems Security Manager (722)		
COMSEC Manager (723)		

Cyberspace IT Work Roles	Primary	Secondary
Technical Support Specialist (411)		
Database Administrator (421)		
Data Analyst (422)		
Knowledge Manager (431)		
Network Operations Specialist (441)		
System Administrator (451)		
Software Developer (621)		
Systems Developer (632)		
Systems Requirements Planner (641)		
Enterprise Architect (651)		
Research and Development Specialist (661)		
System Testing and Evaluation Specialist (671)		

Cyberspace Effects Work Roles	Primary	Secondary
Mission Assessment Specialist (112)		
Exploitation Analyst (121)		
Target Developer (131)		
Target Network Analyst (132)		
Warning Analyst (141)		
Cyber Operations Planner (332)		
Partner Integration Planner (333)		

Cyberspace Intelligence Work Roles	Primary	Secondary
All-Source Analyst (111)		
Multi-Disciplined Language Analyst (151)		
All-Source Collection Manager (311)		
All-Source Collection Requirements Manager (312)		
Cyber Intelligence Planner (331)		

Cyberspace Enablers Work Roles	Primary	Secondary
Forensics Analyst (211)		
Cyber Crime Investigator (221)		
Cyber Instructional Curriculum Developer (711)		
Cyber Instructor (712)		
Cyber Legal Advisor (731)		
Privacy Compliance Manager (732)		
Cyber Workforce Developer and Manager (751)		
Cyber Policy and Strategy Planner (752)		
Program Manager (801)		
IT Project Manager (802)		
Product Support Manager (803)		
IT Investment/Portfolio Manager (804)		
IT Program Auditor (805)		
Executive Cyber Leadership (901)		

Q09

In the table below, please indicate what percentage of your work (out of 100) is dedicated to your primary work role, secondary work role (if applicable), and other tasks in a typical workweek.

	Percentage of Work (0–100)
Primary work role	
Secondary work role	
Other tasks	

Q10

You indicated that none of the cybersecurity or cyberspace IT work roles in the DCWF apply to your current position. Please provide a short description of your current work role in the text box below. (*free-form text field, then send respondent to exit page*)

Frequency of Work Tasks

Q11

For each task associated with your *primary* work role, please read the description and then use the rating scale to indicate how often you perform the task in a typical workweek in your current position.

[*insert selected DCWF tasks, descriptions*]

Task	Never	Yearly	Monthly	Weekly	Daily	Hourly
Work role X, Task title 1 Work role X, Task description 1						
Work role X, Task title 2 Work role X, Task description 2						
... Work role X, Task title *n* Work role X, Task description *n*						

Importance of Work Tasks

Q12

For each task associated with your *primary* work role, [work role X], please read the description and then use the rating scale to indicate how important that task is to successful performance in the typical workweek in your current position in [organization name].

[*insert selected DCWF tasks, descriptions*]

Task	Not Important	Somewhat Important	Important	Very Important	Extremely Important
Work role X, Task title 1 Work role X, Task description 1					
Work role X, Task title 2 Work role X, Task description 2					
... Work role X, Task title *n* Work role X, Task description *n*					

Impacts on Current Work

Q13

Are there changes to policies, programs, practices, or other features of your work environment that would help you perform your current work role more *efficiently* (i.e., leading to the least amount of waste)? If so, what? (*free-form text field*)

Q14

Are there changes to policies, programs, practices, or other features of your work environment that would help you perform your current work role more *effectively* (i.e., successfully producing the desired result)? If so, what? (*free-form text field*)

Additional Background Information

Q15

What is the highest degree or level of education that you have completed?

1. High school diploma/GED
2. Some college credit, but *less* than 1 year of college credit
3. 1 or more years of college credit, no degree
4. Associate degree (for example, AA, AS)
5. Bachelor's degree (for example, BA, BS)
6. Master's degree (for example, MA, MS, MEng, MEd, MSW, MBA)
7. Professional degree beyond a bachelor's degree (for example, MD, DDS, DVM, LLB, JD)
8. Doctoral degree (for example, PhD, EdD)

Q16

What cyber or IT certifications do you hold related to your cybersecurity or cyberspace IT work role? (*free-form text field*)

Q17

What is your gender?

1. Male
2. Female
3. Other/prefer not to say

Q18

Are you Spanish/Hispanic/Latino?

1. No, not Spanish/Hispanic/Latino
2. Yes, Mexican, Mexican American, Chicano, Puerto Rican, Cuban, or other Spanish/Hispanic/Latino

Q19

What is your race? (Mark one or more races to indicate what race you consider yourself to be.)

1. White
2. Black or African American
3. American Indian or Alaska Native
4. Asian (for example, Asian Indian, Chinese, Filipino, Japanese, Korean, or Vietnamese)
5. Native Hawaiian or Other Pacific Islander (for example, Samoan, Guamanian, or Chamorro)
6. Other

APPENDIX C

Deskside Interview Protocol and Example Data Call Results

This appendix reproduces the protocol that we designed to conduct the virtual deskside interviews with selected staff from the organizations selected to participate in the ZBR. At the end of this appendix, we show the data call results for the Network Operations Specialist (441) work role that we shared with deskside interview participants in that work role as an example of what we provided to participants more generally.

Introduction

The FY 2020 National Defense Authorization Act calls for a review of U.S. Department of Defense (DoD) cybersecurity and cyberspace information technology (IT) personnel to be submitted to and jointly reviewed by the Principal Cyber Advisor, the DoD Chief Information Officer, and the Under Secretary of Defense for Personnel and Readiness. RAND's National Defense Research Institute (NDRI) has been asked to conduct research in support of this review. Specifically, RAND NDRI has been asked to validate and ensure the consistency of the data and analysis used by the departments, components, or agencies for organizations submitting reviews.

As part of the RAND NDRI effort, we initially interviewed leadership and supervisors of cybersecurity and cyberspace IT personnel in your organization. Next, a data call was conducted for which members of your organization provided answers based on their cybersecurity or cyberspace IT work role. We analyzed the responses from the data call, and now we are following up with deskside interviews with select individuals in cybersecurity and cyberspace IT work roles to ensure that we interpret the data call findings appropriately.

Specifically, in today's deskside interview, we will ask for your help in reviewing compiled data call results from personnel who indicated that they have the same primary work role as you. We will ask about time spent on certain tasks, the importance of those tasks and other findings related to potential changes in the work role, and how contextual factors, such as the availability of relevant technological tools and systems, affect the work role.

Throughout this discussion, we will refer to the DoD Cyber Workforce Framework (DCWF), which is a taxonomy of work roles that includes specialty areas and tasks for DoD cyber jobs.[1] For definitions of the cybersecurity and cyberspace IT workforces, we reference DoD Directive (DoDD) 8140.01, *Cyberspace Workforce Management*:[2]

> Cybersecurity workforce: Personnel who secure, defend, and preserve data, networks, net-centric capabilities, and other designated systems by ensuring appropriate security controls and measures are in place, and taking internal defense actions. This includes access to system controls, monitoring, administration, and integration of cybersecurity into all aspects of engineering and acquisition of cyberspace capabilities.
>
> Cyberspace IT workforce: Personnel who design, build, configure, operate, and maintain IT, networks, and capabilities. This includes actions to prioritize portfolio investments; architect, engineer, acquire, implement, evaluate, and dispose of IT as well as information resource management; and the management, storage, transmission, and display of data and information.

Participation

Your participation in this discussion is entirely voluntary. You can choose not to participate or skip any points that you would rather not discuss. Additionally, if at any time you no longer want to participate, just let us know, and we can stop the conversation.

How We Will Use the Information That You Provide

During our discussion, we will be taking notes so we can accurately capture your comments for our analyses. In any briefings and reports that we produce, we will combine the information that you provide with information that we receive from other representatives from your organization. We may include some direct quotes in our briefings and reports, but we will not attribute them to anyone by name or in a way that would directly identify you. Please let us know if there is anything that you want us to keep off the record and not quote.

Your name and position will be recorded with the notes that we take and keep in our research files to show that we talked to individuals with critical knowledge and to assist with any follow-up that may be needed. For any briefings and reports that we produce, your name will not be included; however, your position will be included in a list of participants. Are

---

[1] For more information on the DCWF, see DoD Cyber Exchange Public, undated-b. For more information on cybersecurity and cyberspace IT work roles, see DoD Cyber Exchange Public, 2020a; and DoD Cyber Exchange Public, 2020b.

[2] DoDD 8140.01, *Cyberspace Workforce Management*, Washington, D.C.: Office of the DoD Chief Information Officer, October 5, 2020, pp. 11–12.

you comfortable having your position included in a list of participants in our briefings and reports?

Discussion Questions

General Background Questions

First, we would like to ask about your background. This will help us understand the context of your work role relative to your position and work history.

1. Could you start by giving us a brief description of your position and responsibilities?
   a. What is your background and experience prior to your current position?
   b. How long have you been in your current position?
2. Would you please state your primary work role and your secondary work role, if you have one?

Questions About Data Call Results

As we mentioned earlier, we compiled and analyzed the results from the data call that cybersecurity and cyberspace IT professionals in your organization completed. We would like to get your perspective on the results for your primary work role.

We will start by sharing the list of DCWF tasks that correspond with your primary work role.

3. First, we would like to share results for the primary work role tasks by how often they are performed.
   a. Do these results align with your understanding of how often these tasks are typically performed in this work role?
      i. If not, what tasks were reported as being performed more or less frequently than you would expect for this work role? Why?
      ii. What factors (for example, specific technologies) might explain differences in how often these tasks are typically performed in this work role?
   b. To have a better understanding of [selected tasks], can you describe them in your own words and how they fit into what you do in your position?
4. Now, we would like to share results for your primary work role's tasks by how important the task is to successful performance in that work role.
   a. Do these results align with your understanding of how important these tasks are to successful performance in this work role?
      i. If not, what tasks were reported as being more or less important than you would expect for this work role? Why?
      ii. What factors (for example, specific technologies) might affect how important these tasks would typically be for successful performance in this work role?

5. Are there potential shifts in technology, policies, or other kinds of changes in the next five years that would affect your workload?
6. When asked about changes to policies, programs, practices, or other features of the work environment that would help individuals perform their current work role more efficiently (i.e., with the least amount of waste), we heard the following themes: [*insert themes*]
   a. Do you think these would help improve efficiency? Why?
   b. Are there changes to other policies, programs, practices, or other features of the work environment that would help you perform your work role more efficiently? Why?
7. When asked about changes to policies, programs, practices, or other features of the work environment that would help individuals perform their current work role more effectively (i.e., successfully producing the desired result), we heard the following themes: [*insert themes*]
   a. Do you think these would help improve effectiveness? Why?
   b. Are there changes to other policies, programs, practices, or other features of the work environment that would help you perform your work role more effectively? Why?

Closing Questions

8. Is there anything we have not discussed related to your work role(s) that you think we should be aware of as we move forward with our study?
9. Are there relevant reports or materials that you could share with us that might help us better understand your primary work role?

Data Call Results for the Network Operations Specialist (441) Work Role

In this section, we show the data call results for the Network Operations Specialist (441) work role as an example of what we provided to deskside interview participants.

Figures C.1 and C.2 show the core tasks for the Network Operations Specialist (441) that were reported as being performed more frequently and less frequently, respectively. Figures C.3 and C.4 show the core tasks for the Network Operations Specialist (441) that were reported as more important and less important, respectively. Each figure also provides the standard deviation of the task frequency and importance responses. Standard deviations were grouped as follows: less than 1.0 was coded as low, between 1.0 and 1.5 was coded as medium, and greater than 1.5 was coded as high.

FIGURE C.1
Data Call Results for DCWF Work Role 441: More-Frequent Tasks

More-Frequent Tasks

Task	Median frequency	Standard deviation
1. Diagnose network connectivity problem.	4.00	0.88
2. Configure and optimize network hubs, routers, and switches (e.g., higher-level protocols, tunneling).	4.00	1.40
3. Monitor network capacity and performance.	3.50	1.62

Frequency Rating Scale: 0 = never, 1 = yearly, 2 = monthly, 3 = weekly, 4 = daily, 5 = hourly.

Frequency Color Key: How often task is performed

Never | Rarely | Moderately | Often

Standard Deviation Color Key: Response variation level

High | Medium | Low

NOTE: Standard deviations were grouped as follows: less than 1.0 was coded as low, between 1.0 and 1.5 was coded as medium, and greater than 1.5 was coded as high.

FIGURE C.2
Data Call Results for DCWF Work Role 441: Less-Frequent Tasks

Less-Frequent Tasks

Task	Median frequency	Standard deviation
1. Test and maintain network infrastructure including software and hardware devices.	3.00	1.50
2. Patch network vulnerabilities to ensure information is safeguarded against outside parties.	2.00	1.28
3. Install or replace network hubs, routers, and switches.	2.00	0.91
4. Install and maintain network infrastructure device operating system software (e.g., IOS, firmware).	2.00	1.14
5. Develop and implement network backup and recovery procedures.	2.00	1.13

Frequency Rating Scale: 0 = never, 1 = yearly, 2 = monthly, 3 = weekly, 4 = daily, 5 = hourly.

Frequency Color Key: How often task is performed

Never | Rarely | Moderately | Often

Standard Deviation Color Key: Response variation level

High | Medium | Low

NOTE: Standard deviations were grouped as follows: less than 1.0 was coded as low, between 1.0 and 1.5 was coded as medium, and greater than 1.5 was coded as high. IOS = Internetworking Operating System.

FIGURE C.3
Data Call Results for DCWF Work Role 441: More-Important Tasks

More-Important Tasks

Task	Median importance	Standard deviation
1. Diagnose network connectivity problem.	5.00	1.01
2. Patch network vulnerabilities to ensure information is safeguarded against outside parties.	4.00	0.91
3. Monitor network capacity and performance.	4.00	1.32
4. Install or replace network hubs, routers, and switches.	4.00	1.09
5. Install and maintain network infrastructure device operating system software (e.g., IOS, firmware).	4.00	1.08
6. Configure and optimize network hubs, routers, and switches (e.g., higher-level protocols, tunneling).	4.00	1.28
7. Test and maintain network infrastructure including software and hardware devices.	3.50	1.05

Importance Rating Scale: 1 = not important, 2 = somewhat important, 3 = important, 4 = very important, 5 = extremely important.

Importance Color Key: How important task is

Not at all | Moderately | Very/Extremely

Standard Deviation Color Key: Response variation level

High | Medium | Low

NOTE: Standard deviations were grouped as follows: less than 1.0 was coded as low, between 1.0 and 1.5 was coded as medium, and greater than 1.5 was coded as high. IOS = Internetworking Operating System.

FIGURE C.4
Data Call Results for DCWF Work Role 441: Less-Important Tasks

Less-Important Tasks

Task	Median importance	Standard deviation
1. Develop and implement network backup and recovery procedures.	3.00	1.12

Importance Rating Scale: 1 = not important, 2 = somewhat important, 3 = important, 4 = very important, 5 = extremely important.

Importance Color Key: How important task is

Not at all | Moderately | Very/Extremely

Standard Deviation Color Key: Response variation level

High | Medium | Low

NOTE: Standard deviations were grouped as follows: less than 1.0 was coded as low, between 1.0 and 1.5 was coded as medium, and greater than 1.5 was coded as high.

Finally, Figures C.5 and C.6 show the summarized comments from the data call—across all work roles—about efficiency and effectiveness, respectively.

FIGURE C.5
Data Call Results: Efficiency

Comments About Efficiency

Theme	Types of comments
Processes	• Approval of new circuits, manual System Authorization Access Request completion, and compromise isolation • Also, better processes to approve new tools
Personnel	• Shortages lead to "tiger teaming" everything, having non-managers in management roles, and being stretched too thin • Improvements could be made to better codify and clarify duties
Tools	• Varied topics mentioned: redundant systems requiring duplicate reporting efforts; funding/resourcing constraints, faster and better personal computing devices, increased access to internet services, and concerns about specific platforms (e.g., Tanium)
Training	• Spending on security certificates with limited relevance to the work role • Potential imbalance among competing IT/military training requirements

NOTE: Comments are combined across cybersecurity and IT work roles and across all ZBR organizations.

FIGURE C.6
Data Call Results: Effectiveness

Comments About Effectiveness

Theme	Types of comments
Same as efficiency (Personnel, tools processes, training)	• Need for increased personnel, improved computing services, increased desired for telework, and better technical training both for the individual and leadership
Requirements	• Challenges both on the generating (e.g. "I need these things to do my job") and receiving end (e.g. "from other workgroups or from senior leaders")
Roles	• Both specialization and management where greater definition, alignment, and clarity were requested
Newness	• Getting "new" marines up and running • Learning and using new technologies

NOTE: Comments are combined across cybersecurity and IT work roles and across all ZBR organizations.

APPENDIX D

Additional Information on the DoD and Private Sector Cyber Workforce Comparison

In this appendix, we explore the role of workforce mission and environment in staffing considerations. As suggested by the studies that we reviewed, the perception that comparisons with industry (and the subsequent adoption of industry practices) are needed is partly motivated by a common belief that industry "does it better" than DoD organizations. Prior studies, such as those conducted by the U.S. Government Accountability Office (GAO),[1] have shown that private sector firms are able to spend less and employ fewer workers to provide the same or better level of service than DoD, supporting this belief. However, the belief itself should be questioned because it is based on the underlying assumption that the workforce mission and environment of the military (and other federal organizations) is comparable to industry conditions.

Workforce Mission and Environment Differences

Table D.1 suggests some of the differences that may limit the feasibility or effectiveness of DoD adopting industry practices. Rather than not considering practices tainted by these differences outright, we recommend that such considerations be discussed with any changes to process or personnel practices to ensure DoD suitability rather than banking solely on numerical evidence.

For example, compensation is a nontrivial difference distinguishing public and private sector cyber workforces.[2] Burning Glass examined ways that the U.S. government can improve cybersecurity hiring, with specific attention to pay gaps at different levels of seniority. One key finding was that government cybersecurity jobs are four times as likely to ask for a graduate degree even though they pay comparable to entry-level salaries in the private sector and do not pace industry increases in pay for seniority (Markow and Vilvovsky, 2021,

[1] Prior to 2004, GAO was known as the U.S. General Accounting Office. We have spelled out this former name when applicable for citation purposes even though it is essentially the same organization.

[2] Several studies, including Schmidt et al., 2015, and Markow and Vilvovsky, 2021, both suggest that pay alone does not explain all staffing differences.

TABLE D.1

Examples of Workforce Mission and Environment Considerations

	Industry	DoD
Mission		
Consequence of failure	Typically mitigated by diversification of products and services; customer and stakeholder pushback can be short lived.	May result in loss of life, national power, or public trust.
Diversity of competencies	Focuses on many aspects of a main product line.[a]	Required to handle DOTMLPF aspects on many operating domains and objectives.
Measures of success	Determined quantitatively in terms of revenue, number of customers, or perceived value.	Specific to the objective and generally narrative based; competing demands of success from external sources.
Planning for contingency[b]	Exists in a demand dynamic but fundamentally peaceful and stable market.	Exists in peaceful competition but must be able to escalate and operate in a conflict situation.
Environment		
Compensation	Driven by labor market and/or internal demand; additional nonmonetary incentives.	Limited by federal regulations and hiring practices.
Flexibility	Ability to shift personnel to suit business or personal needs; focused job title and practices allow opportunity for skill growth.	Uniformed and civilian personnel tend to have other duties and responsibility; less opportunity for skill growth and diversification driven by primary job descriptions.
Sensitivity	Ability to hire diverse staffing with less regard to background; flexible work options because of unclassified nature.	Must meet U.S. citizenship and other background requirements; classified tools and networks require on-premises workforce.
Location	Ability to centralize operations for efficiency.	Globally and dynamically distributed supported workforce; some locations driven by non-business reasons.

NOTE: Examples are not specific to the cyber workforce. DOTMLPF = doctrine, organization, training, materiel, leadership and education, personnel, and facilities.

[a] Some private sector companies have adopted a conglomerate organization, but each entity still tends to focus on a main product line.

[b] DoD has shifted significant focus to operations during competition, a relatively peaceful phase of military operations. This does not eliminate the need for military forces to plan for contingency operations, typically marked by armed conflict.

pp. 8, 16). Perhaps not surprisingly, this 2021 study also revealed retention issues, concluding that 27 percent of new hires leave within their first year (Markow and Vilvovsky, 2021, p. 13).

Organizational differences also inform how public and private sectors staff their cyber workforces. Burning Glass found that cybersecurity jobs in the private sector are 87 percent more likely than government cybersecurity jobs to demand cutting-edge skills and suggested that government positions value this talent less (Markow and Vilvovsky, 2021, p. 7). Participants in our work analysis data call similarly spoke of the lack of incentives or processes in place to enable employee opportunities to develop skills.

Schmidt et al., 2015, demonstrates the challenges to making these comparisons, specifically in terms of identifying "best practices" and attempting a one-to-one comparison. The difficulties that those researchers experienced in studying industry and Air Force workforces suggest that approaching a similar question for all of DoD, as this study was tasked with attempting, would be difficult. The earlier study noted that some effective practices are limited only to certain contexts or best suited to a particular company or organization and not generalizable (Schmidt et al., 2015, p. 5). This point underscores our assertion that comparing the DoD's manning with industry requires a more holistic approach that was beyond the scope and resources of this project.

Cyber Personnel Literature Review

This section provides an overview of our efforts to review literature examining DoD cyber personnel related to comparisons between DoD and private sector workforces.

The Marine Corps conducted one of the few quantitative ZBRs that concluded in FY 2019 assessing whether (1) the Marine Corps cyber workforce had the right staffing and skill sets and (2) whether it was organized effectively to support the cyber mission. Regarding the first objective, the Marine Corps ZBR used a combination of analytical techniques, from reviewing organizational structure and staffing rosters to estimating workload, assessing personnel inventory relative to specific skills, and benchmarking performance measures against those found in private industry.[3]

Ultimately, the Marine Corps ZBR identified areas where cyber staff were lacking—in number, or skill set, or both—and some misalignment of organizations contributing to the cyber mission across the enterprise (Mallory and Logan, 2020). Instead of recommending a defined increase or reallocation of personnel to the cybersecurity and IT workforces, the Marine Corps ZBR culminated in recommendations that mapped to four lines of effort: governance (establish an enterprise IT governance model), people (invest in training for the IT workforce), processes (develop mature IT service management processes), and technology (develop a full life-cycle infrastructure technology plan). These four lines of effort were

[3] Such measures might include data storage usage and service desk task frequency and resolution time (Mallory and Logan, 2020).

intended to shape how the Marine Corps delivered cyber services more closely to industry standard practices.[4]

In addition, only a small body of past work exists comparing the allocation of DoD staffing to industry , and fewer efforts that specifically compare allocation of cybersecurity or IT personnel. For example, a 1998 report compares federal (including DoD) and private sector budgeting for IT functions, identifying some IT functions where savings could be realized, but it did not provide a detailed analysis as to how those functions were staffed (U.S. General Accounting Office, 1998). Other GAO reports discuss cybersecurity and IT service implementation and people strategies intended to mimic industry best practices.[5] These reports solicited practices from private companies which are similar in size and purpose to federal agencies (including DoD) and assess the progress that each federal agency is making in implementing these practices. Although these reports acknowledge that discussion of an appropriate mix of cyber personnel is needed to have an effective workforce, they stop short of drawing quantitative comparisons in terms of personnel requirements, both in mix and absolute number (GAO, 2011, 2016, 2019).[6] Although the NDAA requires a revisit to this topic, the value of capturing and applying industry practices has not been ignored by Congress, illustrated during a 2010 hearing that solicited private sector perspectives on DoD cybersecurity and IT (U.S. House of Representatives, 2010). However, these testimonies also omitted any quantitative comparison or specific metrics with which DoD could benchmark their workforce against industry standards.

Other reports highlight hiring, retention, and compensation differences between industry and DoD, further demonstrating key differences between the two workforces (DoD Cyber Exchange Public, undated-a).[7] For example, Knapp et al., 2021, leverages the NICE framework (on which portions of the DCWF is based)[8] to describe the workforce composition but finds that a standard crosswalk between NICE work roles and BLS work role codes does not exist.

Schmidt et al., 2015, examines private sector practices to inform Air Force cybersecurity and IT planning and operations. This report includes one explicit workforce sizing metric,

---

4 The Information Technology Infrastructure Library (ITIL) is an evolving set of IT practices, standards, and certifications initially created by the British government's Central Computer and Telecommunications Agency and is now administered by Axelos as ITIL 4®. For more information, see IBM Cloud Education, 2019, and Axelos, undated.

5 *People strategy* includes traditional talent management roles, such as recruitment and retention, as well as individual improvement and targeted employment to meet specific business needs.

6 Relatedly, U.S. General Accounting Office, 2001, specifically draws recommendations from how industry outsources IT functions but also does not draw quantitative conclusions about the number of personnel or skills needed to adequately provide IT services to organizations of a specific size or function.

7 RAND reports include Libicki, Senty, and Pollak, 2014 (which primarily focuses on cybersecurity) and Knapp et al., 2021. Hattiangadi, 2001 (a CNA report) includes a related Navy-specific analysis on private sector benefits that aggregates all professional fields.

8 See DoDD 8140.01, 2020 for the directive that established the DCWF.

suggesting that "[commercial sector] ratios show 95 percent of the cyber workforce engaged in IT and 5 percent in [information security]," but it also recommends "a workforce study to determine the appropriate ratio" (Schmidt et al., 2015, p. xvi).[9]

CompTIA, a professional organization, provides both cybersecurity and IT certifications, as well as annual reports that forecast the future needs of the commercial cyber workforce (CompTIA, 2020). These annual reports are less transparent in their survey methodology, but they provide broad insights about industry trends before inferring future needs for "critical [skill] areas" in infrastructure, software development, and cybersecurity. Duplicated in Figure D.1, these critical areas are also not aligned to DCWF or NICE but suggest the type of roles that commercial firms are focused on to meet future cybersecurity and IT needs.

Likewise, $(ISC)^2$, a cybersecurity professional organization that offers industry standard certifications, periodically publishes studies that reveal extant and desired characteristics of the cybersecurity workforce ($(ISC)^2$, 2019, 2020, 2021).[10] Its 2020 study uses a survey methodology to reflect the current and an ideal mix (where *ideal* was determined by respondents' subjective view of proper allocation) of cybersecurity team roles, as shown in Figure D.2. The 2021 $(ISC)^2$ study breaks from the 2020 study by identifying how the surveyed global workforce aligns to the NICE framework (as shown in Figure D.3) instead of to team roles. Comparing this with the ZBR data is not straightforward because not all NICE specialty areas were surveyed during the ZBR, and more granular data from the $(ISC)^2$ study was not made available. The report does conclude that the training infrastructure is unable to keep pace with the increasing ubiquity of IT and the growing sophistication of cyber threats ($(ISC)^2$, 2021).[11]

Note that although both CompTIA and $(ISC)^2$ provide insight into the staffing challenges, needs, and demographics of IT and cybersecurity work roles, they do not use work role titles that align to the DCWF or NICE roles, nor do they provide context about the industries that the IT departments in their samples are servicing. Other studies are similarly limited because DCWF workforce elements and NICE specialty areas do not map easily to job titles or occupational codes used by various data collection groups. For example, Gartner conducts proprietary research that leverages private sector relationships to build cybersecurity and IT benchmarks that quantify industry norms for specific role staff-

---

[9] When soliciting practices from the private sector, participants were asked to describe the cyber mission areas in which the company engaged in the NICE framework lexicon. Broad recommendations from the report included increasing the size of the cybersecurity workforce, limiting outsourcing, and managing cybersecurity (which they labeled information security) and IT as separate career fields.

[10] $(ISC)^2$ is considered "vendor-neutral," meaning that the certifications it offers and the surveys that it conducts are not specific to a branded solution, such as Red Hat or Microsoft.

[11] Reflecting on the study's finding, Joseph Marks of the *Washington Post* stated, "Here's the problem in a nutshell: Hacking threats have grown precipitously during the past quarter century as Internet technology has become indispensable to businesses and individuals. But the academic infrastructure to train cyber pros is comparatively in its infancy" (Marks, 2021).

FIGURE D.1
Comparison of CompTIA IT Industry Outlook Critical Area Forecasts, 2020

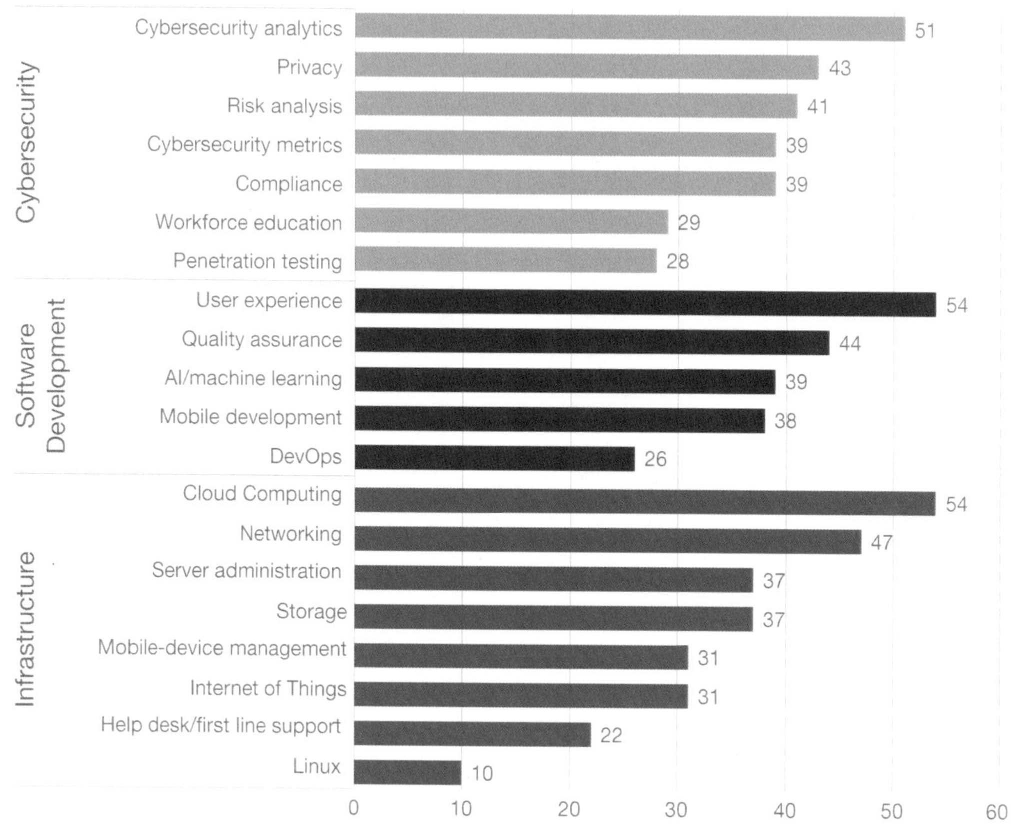

SOURCE: CompTIA, 2020.
NOTE: Identified critical areas are not explicitly aligned to DCWF or NICE work roles. Percentages indicate the portion of firms among all respondents that identified the area as critical.

ing, generally referred to as IT key metrics data products.[12] These benchmarks identify staffing and spending distributions based on industry, revenue size, and work roles (though again, the work roles do not align to the DCWF). Despite the limitations described above, we were still able to conduct a broad comparison between private sector and DoD organizations for the work roles examined in the DoD cyber ZBR.

[12] See Stegman et al., 2020, as an example. Although some Gartner publications are available to the public, such documents often focus on high-level recommendations concerning process or organization. Reports that may be applicable to answering the NDAA questions typically contain client-privileged information that is not easily disseminated.

FIGURE D.2
Comparison of Ideal and Current Mixes of Cybersecurity Team Roles, 2020

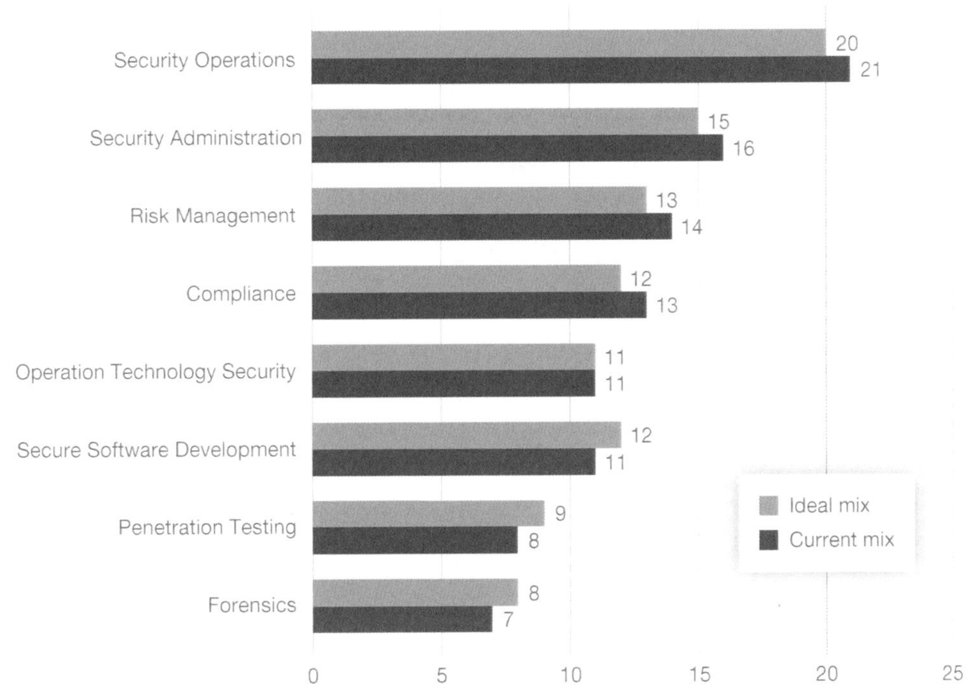

SOURCE: (ISC)², 2020.

NOTE: Percentages indicate the current or ideal average percentage of specific roles that should comprise a cybersecurity team.

FIGURE D.3
Global Cyber Workforce Alignment with NICE Specialty Areas, 2021

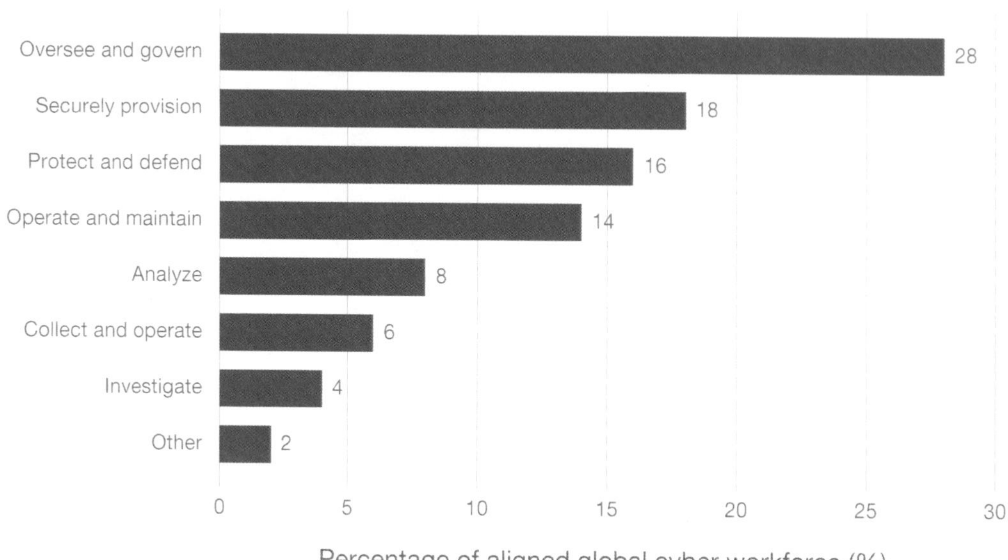

SOURCE: (ISC)², 2021.
NOTE: Percentages indicate the alignment of the global cyber workforce to NICE specialty areas. The original figure did not sum to 100 percent.

Burning Glass Comparison Data (Tabular)

Table D.2 is a tabular version of Figure 3.18 in which we compare private and public sector job posting data from Burning Glass with information on workforce gaps collected during the ZBR.

TABLE D.2
Comparison of Cyber Work Role Demand with ZBR-Surveyed Work Roles

DCWF Work Role	ZBR Organizations (%)	CyberSeek–Public Sector (%)	CyberSeek–Private Sector (%)
Cybersecurity			
(212) Cyber Defense Forensics Analyst	1	3	2
(461) Systems Security Analyst	2	13	11
(511) Cyber Defense Analyst	0 (–13)	3	3
(521) Cyber Defense Infrastructure Support Specialist	5	5	6
(531) Cyber Defense Incident Responder	1	5	5
(541) Vulnerability Assessment Analyst	2	7	7
(611) Authorizing Official/Designating Representative	0	1	2
(612) Security Control Assessor	2	5	6
(622) Secure Software Assessor	0 (18)	2	2
(631) Information Systems Sec. Developer	2	3	3
(652) Security Architect	0 (16)	4	6
(722) Information Systems Security Manager	4	3	4
(723) COMSEC Manager	1	1	0 (1,820)
IT			
(411) Technical Support Specialist	25	7	3
(421) Database Administrator	2	3	3
(422) Data Analyst	1	4	4
(431) Knowledge Manager	2	2	3
(441) Network Operations Specialist	9	6	6
(451) System Administrator	12	8	7
(621) Software Developer	9	6	8
(632) Systems Developer	6	5	6
(641) Systems Requirements Planner	4	2	2
(651) Enterprise Architect	2	0 (212)	0 (5,639)
(661) Research and Development Specialist	4	0 (269)	0 (2,097)
(671) System Testing and Evaluation Specialist	4	2	1

SOURCE: Authors' analysis of April 2020 to March 2021 NIST data (CyberSeek, undated), as well as distribution list data collected from the selected DoD organizations.

NOTE: Percentages represent counts of a specific work role divided by all work roles listed. Parenthetical values beside 0 percent values represent the total count in a specific work role; negative numbers indicate a surplus of personnel in that work role. The ZBR survey produced a total of 3,951 entries; CyberSeek–Public Sector had 81,157 entries; and CyberSeek–Private Sector had 1,171,327 entries.

APPENDIX E

Median Task Frequency and Importance for Specific Work Roles

Figures E.1–E.10 show median task frequency and importance for ten work roles that were featured in the organization-level analyses that we provided directly to the services and DISA but were not shown in Chapter Three. Recall that in the DCWF, tasks are referred to as KSATs, which are denoted in the following figures by a three- or four-digit code.[1] Additionally, many tasks have the same median values for task frequency and importance, and therefore one block may be labeled with multiple KSAT codes. Finally, although we do not show variation among the selected organizations in these figures, we did provide such information directly to the services and DISA.

[1] For a more complete list of KSATs for cybersecurity and cyberspace IT work roles, see DoD Cyber Exchange Public, 2020a; and DoD Cyber Exchange Public, 2020b.

FIGURE E.1
Median Task Frequency and Importance, by KSAT, for Systems Security Analyst (461) Across All Selected Organizations

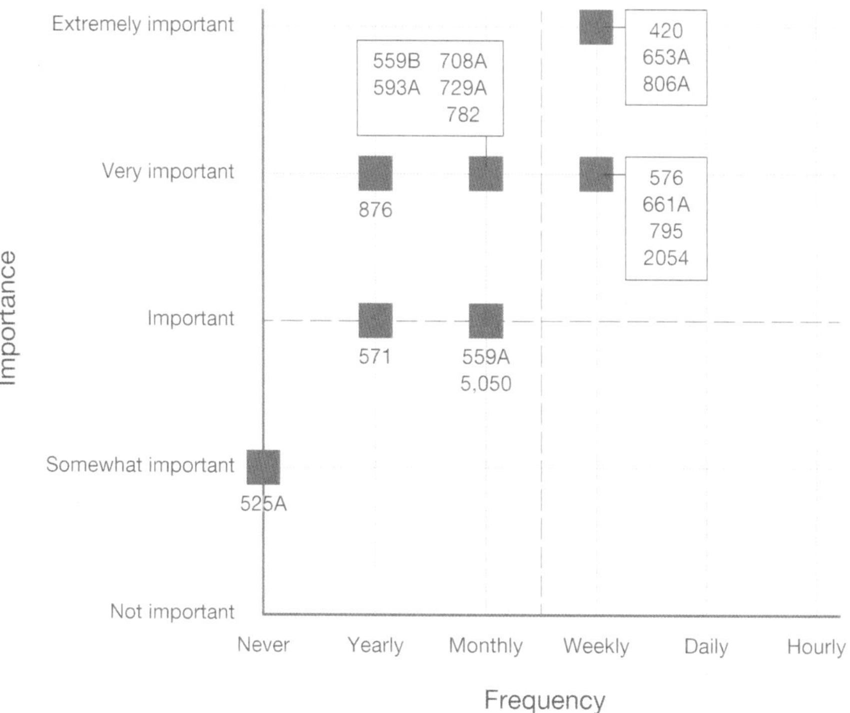

NOTE: Tasks are labeled according to KSAT code, per the DCWF taxonomy (DoD Cyber Exchange Public, 2020a). $n = 17$.

FIGURE E.2

Median Task Frequency and Importance, by KSAT, for Cyber Defense Infrastructure Support Specialist (521) Across All Selected Organizations

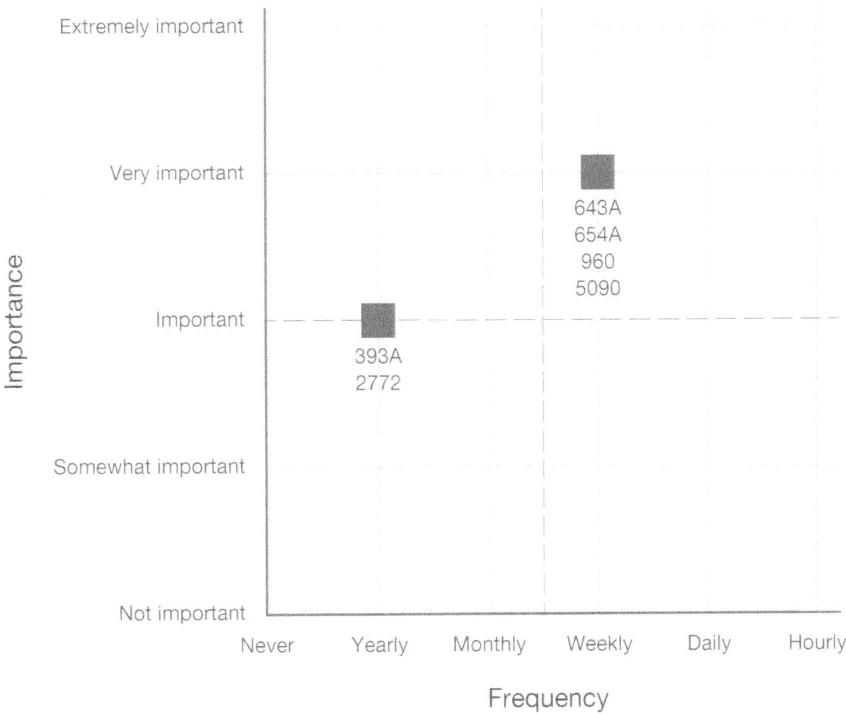

NOTE: Tasks are labeled according to KSAT code, per the DCWF taxonomy (DoD Cyber Exchange Public, 2020a). *n* = 20.

FIGURE E.3

Median Task Frequency and Importance, by KSAT, for Vulnerability Assessment Analyst (541) Across All Organizations

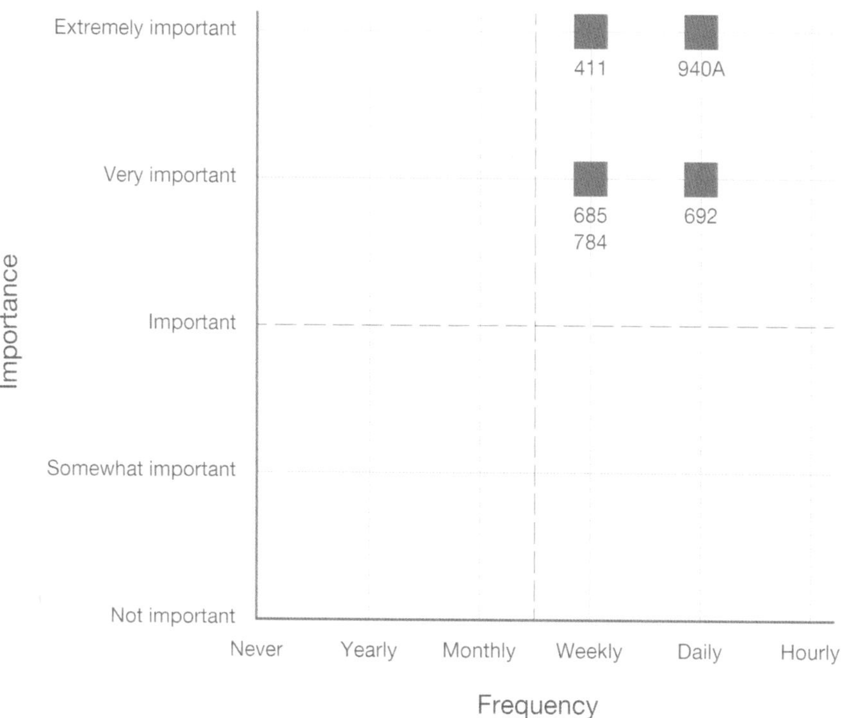

NOTE: Tasks are labeled according to KSAT code, per the DCWF taxonomy (DoD Cyber Exchange Public, 2020a). $n = 41$.

FIGURE E.4
Median Task Frequency and Importance, by KSAT, for Security Control Assessor (612) Across All Selected Organizations

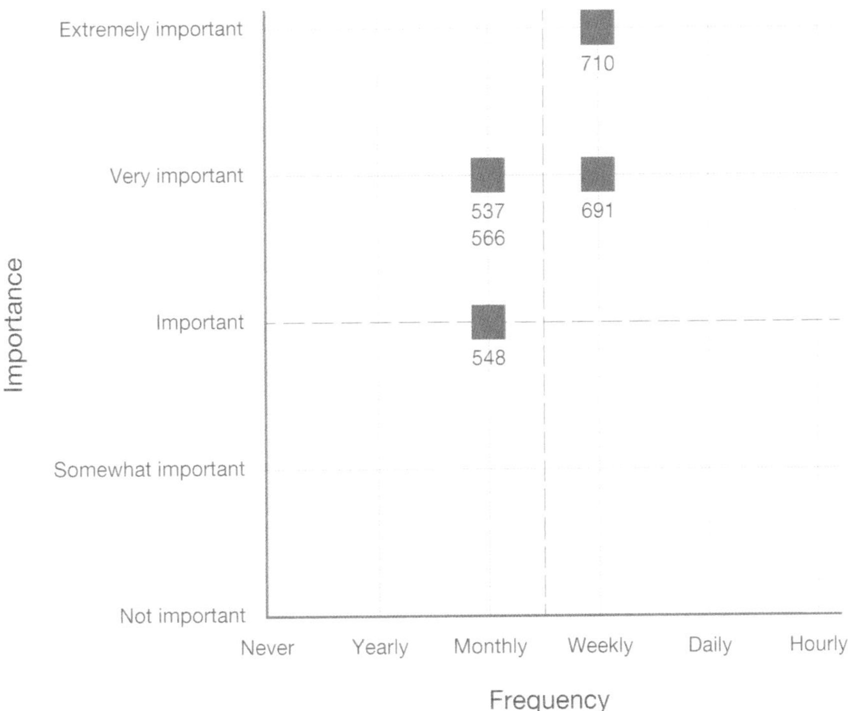

NOTE: Tasks are labeled according to KSAT code, per the DCWF taxonomy (DoD Cyber Exchange Public, 2020a). n = 29.

FIGURE E.5
Median Task Frequency and Importance, by KSAT, for Database Administrator (421) Across All Selected Organizations

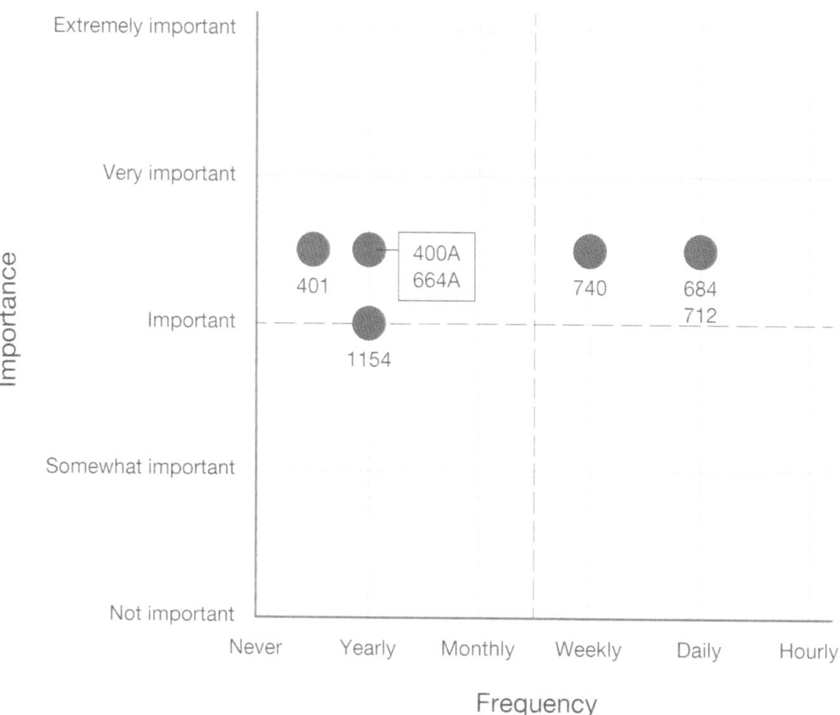

NOTE: Tasks are labeled according to KSAT code, per the DCWF taxonomy (DoD Cyber Exchange Public, 2020a). $n = 4$.

FIGURE E.6
Median Task Frequency and Importance, by KSAT, for Software Developer (621) Across All Selected Organizations

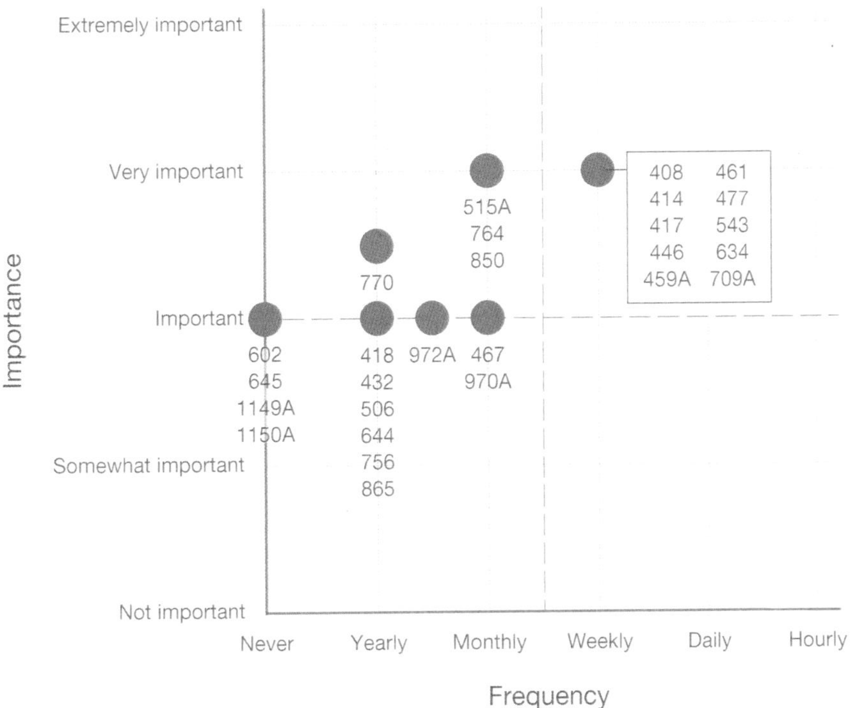

NOTE: Tasks are labeled according to KSAT code, per the DCWF taxonomy (DoD Cyber Exchange Public, 2020a). n = 100.

FIGURE E.7
Median Task Frequency and Importance, by KSAT, for Systems Developer (632) Across All Selected Organizations

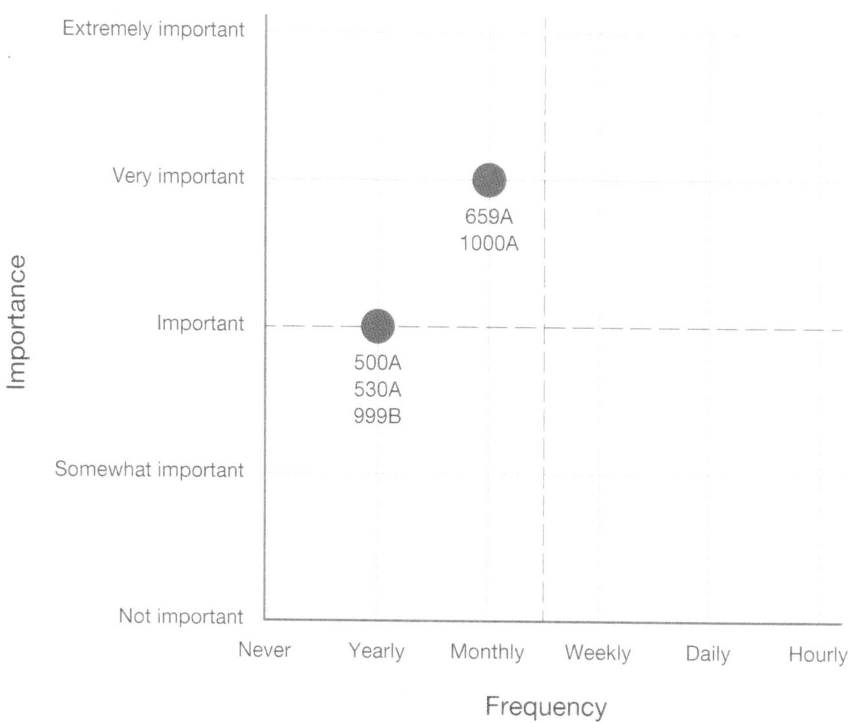

NOTE: Tasks are labeled according to KSAT code, per the DCWF taxonomy (DoD Cyber Exchange Public, 2020a). $n = 23$.

FIGURE E.8
Median Task Frequency and Importance, by KSAT, for Systems Requirements Planner (641) Across All Selected Organizations

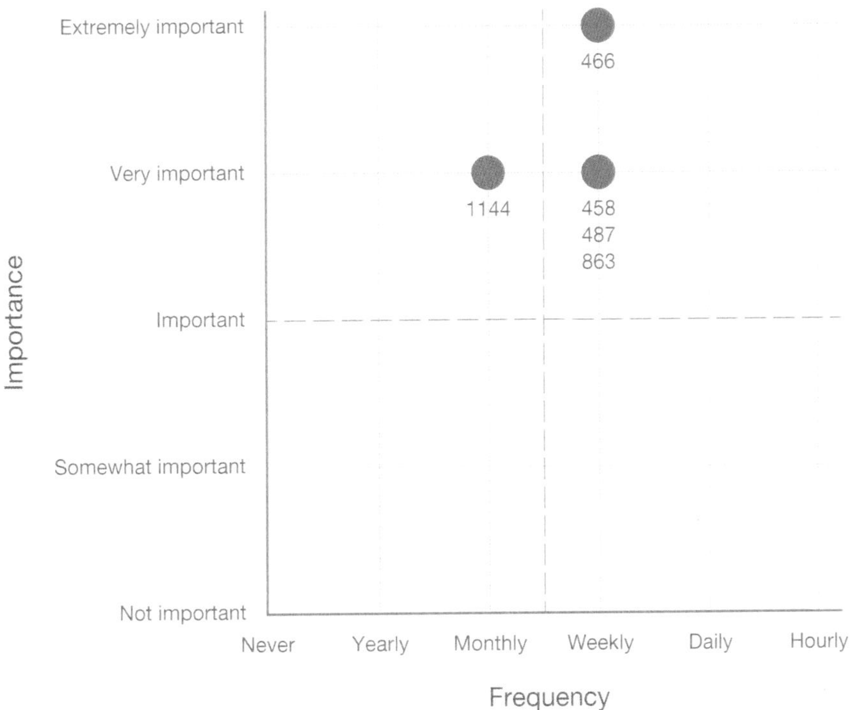

NOTE: Tasks are labeled according to KSAT code, per the DCWF taxonomy (DoD Cyber Exchange Public, 2020a). $n = 52$.

FIGURE E.9

Median Task Frequency and Importance, by KSAT, for Enterprise Architect (651) Across All Selected Organizations

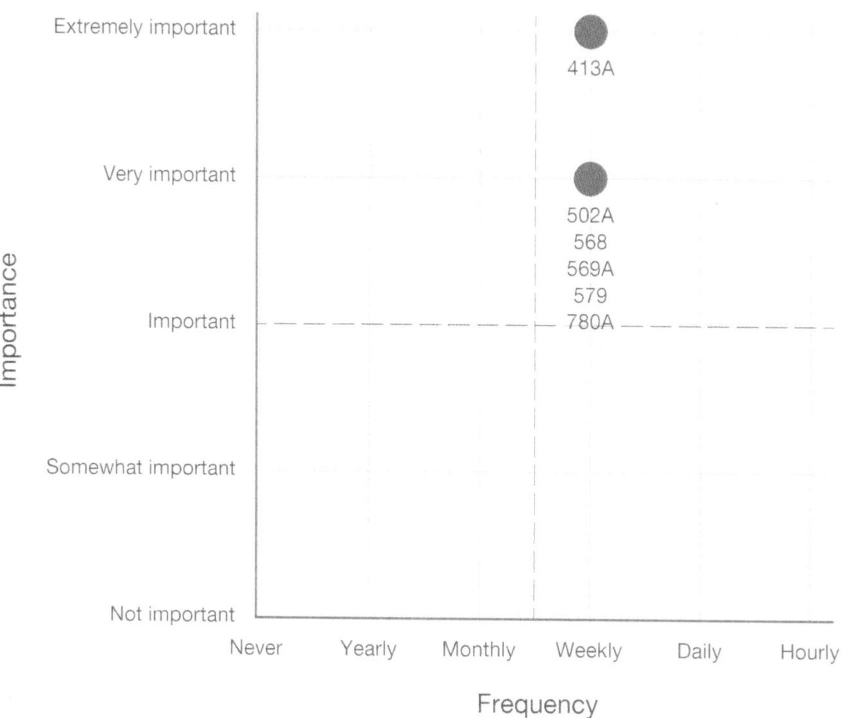

NOTE: Tasks are labeled according to KSAT code, per the DCWF taxonomy (DoD Cyber Exchange Public, 2020a). $n = 64$.

FIGURE E.10
Median Task Frequency and Importance, by KSAT, for System Testing and Evaluation Specialist (671) Across All Selected Organizations

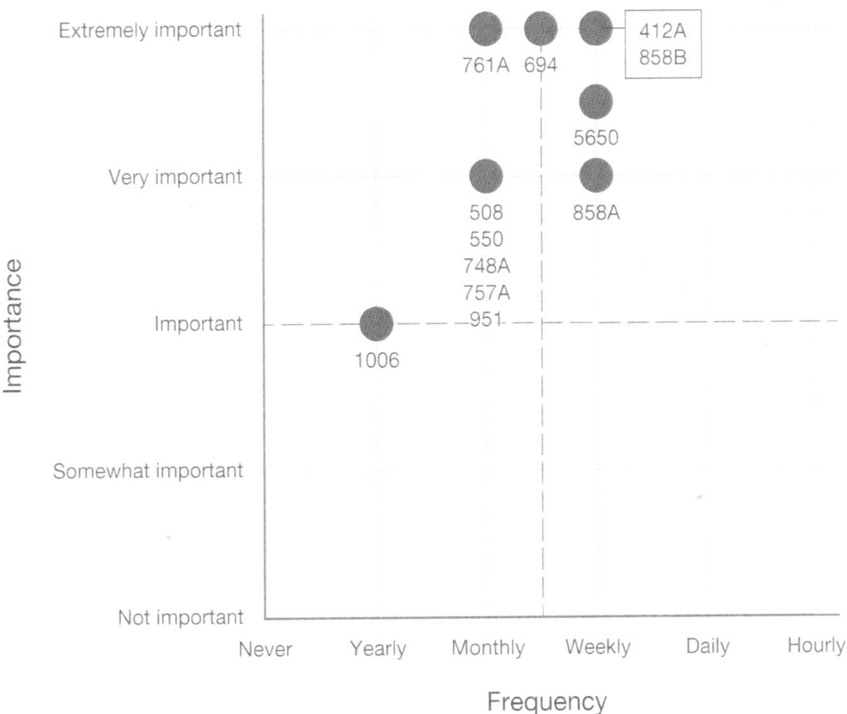

NOTE: Tasks are labeled according to KSAT code, per the DCWF taxonomy (DoD Cyber Exchange Public, 2020a). n = 102.

Abbreviations

1st Network Bn	1st Network Battalion
AO	action officer
BLS	U.S. Bureau of Labor Statistics
COMSEC	communications security
DCWF	DoD Cyber Workforce Framework
DISA	Defense Information Systems Agency
DoD	U.S. Department of Defense
DoD CIO	Department of Defense, Chief Information Officer
DoDM	Department of Defense Manual
FY	fiscal year
GAO	U.S. Government Accountability Office
IT	information technology
ITIL	Information Technology Infrastructure Library
JFHQ-DODIN	Joint Force Headquarters–Department of Defense Information Network
KSAT	knowledge, skills, abilities, and tasks
MCIWEST	Marine Corps Installations West
NAICS	North American Industry Classification System
NDAA	National Defense Authorization Act
NICE	National Initiative for Cybersecurity Education
PCA	Principal Cyber Advisor
PD	position description
SME	subject-matter expert
SOC	standard occupational code
USD P&R	Under Secretary of Defense for Personnel and Readiness
ZBB	zero-based budgeting
ZBR	zero-based review

References

Alarcon, Gene M., "A Meta-Analysis of Burnout with Job Demands, Resources, and Attitudes," *Journal of Vocational Behavior*, Vol. 79, No. 2, October 2011, pp. 549–562.

Axelos, "What Is ITIL?" webpage, undated. As of September 1, 2021:
https://www.axelos.com/certifications/itil-service-management/what-is-itil

Bennett, Darrel Laham Winston, and Thomas K. Landauer, Jr., "An LSA-Based Software Tool for Matching Jobs, People, and Instruction," *Interactive Learning Environments*, Vol. 8, No. 3, December 2000, pp. 171–185.

BLS—*See* U.S. Bureau of Labor Statistics.

Braun, Virginia, and Victoria Clarke, "Using Thematic Analysis in Psychology," *Qualitative Research in Psychology*, Vol. 3, No. 2, 2006, pp. 77–101.

CompTIA, *IT Industry Outlook 2021: Rebuilding for the Future*, Downers Grove, Ill., November 2020.

———, email discussion with the authors to address questions about the cybersecurity heat map, October 5, 2021.

CyberSeek, homepage, undated. As of October 1, 2021:
https://www.cyberseek.org/

Daniels, Seamus P., *Understanding DoD's Defense-Wide Zero-Based Review*, Washington D.C.: Center for Strategic and International Studies, September 2019.

Department of Defense Directive 8140.01, *Cyberspace Workforce Management*, Washington, D.C.: Office of the DoD Chief Information Officer, October 5, 2020.

Department of Defense Manual 8570.01, *Information Assurance Workforce Improvement Program*, incorporating change 4, Washington, D.C.: Assistant Secretary of Defense for Networks and Information Integration, Department of Defense Chief Information Officer, November 10, 2015.

DoD—*See* U.S. Department of Defense.

DoDD—*See* Department of Defense Directive.

DoDM—*See* Department of Defense Manual.

DoD Cyber Exchange Public, "DoD Cyber Workforce Framework," webpage, undated-a. As of September 1, 2021:
https://public.cyber.mil/cw/dcwf/

———,"Workforce Elements," webpage, undated-b. As of March 1, 2021:
https://public.cyber.mil/cw/dcwf/workforce-elements/

———,"Workforce Elements: Cybersecurity," webpage, May 28, 2020a. As of March 1, 2021:
https://public.cyber.mil/wf-element-sub/cybersecurity/

———,"Workforce Elements: IT (Cyberspace)," webpage, May 28, 2020b. As of March 1, 2021:
https://public.cyber.mil/wf-element-sub/it-cyberspace/

GAO—*See* U.S. Government Accountability Office.

Glaser, Barney G., and Anselm L. Strauss, *The Discovery of Grounded Theory: Strategies for Qualitative Research*, New Brunswick, N.J.: Transaction Publishers, AldineTransaction, 1967.

Hattiangadi, Anita U., *Private-Sector Benefit Offerings in the Competition for High-Skill Recruits*, CRM D0003564.A2 FINAL, Alexandria, Va.: CNA Corporation, December 2001.

IBM Cloud Education, "IT Infrastructure Library (ITIL)," webpage, May 22, 2019. As of September 1, 2021:
https://www.ibm.com/cloud/learn/it-infrastructure-library

(ISC)[2], *Strategies for Building and Growing Strong Cybersecurity Teams: (ISC)[2] Cybersecurity Workforce Study, 2019*, Clearwater, Fla., 2019.

———,*Cybersecurity Professional Stand Up to a Pandemic: (ISC)[2] Cybersecurity Workforce Study, 2020*, Clearwater, Fla., 2020.

———,*A Resilient Cybersecurity Profession Charts the Path Forward: (ISC)[2] Cybersecurity Workforce Study, 2021*, Clearwater, Fla., 2021.

Knapp, David, Sina Beaghley, Troy D. Smith, Molly F. McIntosh, Karen Schwindt, Norah Griffin, Daniel Schwam, and Hanna Hoover, *DoD Cyber Excepted Service Labor Market Analysis and Options for Use of Compensation Flexibilities*, Santa Monica, Calif.: RAND Corporation, RR-A730-1, 2021. As of September 1, 2021:
https://www.rand.org/pubs/research_reports/RRA730-1.html

Libicki, Martin C., David Senty, and Julia Pollak, *Hackers Wanted: An Examination of the Cybersecurity Labor Market*, Santa Monica, Calif.: RAND Corporation, RR-430, 2014. As of September 1, 2021:
https://www.rand.org/pubs/research_reports/RR430.html

Mallory, Christine, and Brent Logan, "USMC ZBR Overview and Lessons Learned," presentation, Washington D.C.: Cyber Advisory Group, May 7, 2020, Not available to the general public.

Markow, William, and Nomi Vilvovsky, *Securing a Nation: Improving Federal Cybersecurity Hiring in the United States*, Boston, Mass.: Burning Glass Technologies, March 2021.

Marks, Joseph, "The U.S. Cyber Workforce Gap Is Getting Bigger," *Washington Post*, October 26, 2021.

MAX.gov, homepage, undated. As of November 1, 2020:
https://portal.max.gov/portal/home

Morgeson, Frederick P., and Erich C. Dierdorff, "Work Analysis: From Technique to Theory," in Sheldon Zedeck, ed., *APA Handbook of Industrial and Organizational Psychology*, Vol. 2: *Selecting and Developing Members for the Organization*, Washington, D.C.: American Psychological Association, 2011, pp. 3–41.

National Institute of Standards and Technology, "The Workforce Framework for Cybersecurity (NICE Framework): Supplemental Material," webpage, April 19, 2022. As of September 1, 2021:
https://www.nist.gov/itl/applied-cybersecurity/nice/nice-framework-resource-center/workforce-framework-cybersecurity-nice

Navy Cyber ZBR Task Force, *Navy Cyber Workforce Zero-Based Review*, Washington, D.C., April 2012, Not available to the general public.

Newhouse, William, Stephanie Keith, Benjamin Scribner, and Greg Witte, *National Initiative for Cybersecurity Education (NICE): Cybersecurity Workforce Framework*, Gaithersburg, Md.: National Institute of Standards and Technology, NIST SP 800-181, August 2017.

NIST—*See* National Institute of Standards and Technology.

Office of Management and Budget, *Standard Occupational Classification Manual: United States, 2018*, Washington, D.C.: Executive Office of the President, 2018.

Office of the Secretary of Defense, *Report to Congress: FY2021 Defense Wide Review*, Secretary of Defense, Washington, D.C.: U.S. Department of Defense, January 2020.

Petersen, Rodney, Danielle Santos, Matthew C. Smith, Karen A. Wetzel, and Greg Witte, *Workforce Framework for Cybersecurity (NICE Framework)*, Gaithersburg, Md.: National Institute of Standards and Technology, NIST SP 800-181 revision 1, November 2020.

Public Law 116-92, National Defense Authorization Act for Fiscal Year 2020, December 20, 2019.

Pyhrr, Peter A., "Zero-Base Budgeting," *Harvard Business Review*, Vol. 48, No. 6, November/December 1970, pp. 111–121.

Schmidt, Lara, Caolionn O'Connell, Hirokazu Miyake, Akhil R. Shah, Joshua William Baron, Geof Nieboer, Rose Jourdan, David Senty, Zev Winkelman, Louise Taggart, Susanne Sondergaard, and Neil Robinson, *Cyber Practices: What Can the U.S. Air Force Learn from the Commercial Sector?* Santa Monica, Calif.: RAND Corporation, RR-847-AF, 2015. As of September 1, 2021:
https://www.rand.org/pubs/research_reports/RR847.html

Stegman, Eric, Jamie Gueveara, Nick Michelogiannakis, Shreya Futela, Sneha Sharma, and Shaivya Kaushal, *IT Key Metrics Data 2021: Industry Measures—Cross-Industry Analysis*, Stamford, Conn.: Gartner, ID G00737592, December 18, 2020.

U.S. Bureau of Labor Statistics, "Occupational Employment and Wage Statistics," webpage, undated. As of September 1, 2021:
https://www.bls.gov/oes/

U.S. Department of Defense, "FY2020 National Defense Authorization Act §1652 Zero-Based Review (ZBR) of the Cyber Workforce: Courses of Action for Reduced Scope," presentation, Washington, D.C.: Department of Defense Chief Information Officer, May 2020, Not available to the general public.

U.S. General Accounting Office, *Federal Productivity: DOD Functions with Savings Potential from Private Sector Cost Comparisons*, Washington, D.C., GAO/GGD-88-63FS, April 1998.

———,*Information Technology: Leading Commercial practices for Outsourcing of Services*, Washington, D.C., GAO-02-214, November 2001.

U.S. Government Accountability Office, *Cybersecurity Human Capital: Initiatives Need Better Planning and Coordination*, Washington, D.C., GAO-12-8, November 2011.

———, *IT Workforce: Key Practices Help Ensure Strong Integrated Program Teams; Selected Departments Need to Assess Skill Gaps*, Washington, D.C., GAO-17-8, November 2016.

———,*Information Technology: Agencies Need to Fully Implement Key Workforce Planning Activities*, Washington, D.C., GAO-20-129, October 2019.

U.S. House of Representatives, *Private Sector Perspectives on Department of Defense Information Technology and Cybersecurity Activities: Hearing Before the Subcommittee on Terrorism, Unconventional Threats and Capabilities of the Committee on Armed Services*, Washington, D.C.: U.S. Government Printing Office, February 25, 2010.

Vintun, "United States Marine Corps Zero-Based Review: Consolidated Current State Assessment," Alexandria, Va., M67854-17-C-4441, July 19, 2019a, Not available to the general public.

———,"United States Marine Corps Zero-Based Review (ZBR): Target Future State," Alexandria, Va., M67854-17-C-4441, August 9, 2019b, Not available to the general public.

———,"USMC IT Workforce Zero-Based Review: Preparing for the Target Future State Workshop," presentation, Alexandria, Va., August 13, 2019c, Not available to the general public.